Together for Past and Present

معًا من أجل الماضي والحاضر

Cultural Heritage
Collaborations
between the
United States
and Jordan
on the
75th Anniversary
of
Their
Bilateral Relations

أوجه التعاون
في إحياء الإرث الثقافي
بين
الولايات المتحدة الأميركية
و المملكة الأردنية الهاشمية
بمناسبة
الذكرى الخامسة والسبعين
لإرساء
العلاقات الثنائية المتبادلة

The American Center of Research
Amman, Jordan — Alexandria, Virginia

This book and accompanying exhibit have been made possible with a generous grant from the United States Embassy in Amman.

In addition to the individuals and organizations who provided the images in this book, thanks are due to the following, who contributed notes for the text:

Russell B. Adams
Pierre and Patricia Bikai
Douglas Clark
Geoffrey Hedges-Knyrim
Jehad Haron
Jenna de Vries Morton
Øystein S. LaBianca
Konstantine Politis
Barbara A. Porter
Edward Prados
Suzanne Richard
Gary Rollefson
Yorke Rowan

Additional assistance with the text was provided by the staff of the United States Embassy in Amman.

Assistance with obtaining and identifying images was graciously provided by Hala Al Syouf, head librarian of the Department of Antiquities; Maram Mazahreh, art director of the Jordan Tourism Board; Dina Al Majali, archive assistant, ACOR; and the staff of the United States Embassy in Amman.

Selection and text by Pearce Paul Creasman and Shatha Abu Aballi.

Arabic translation by Shatha Abu Aballi and Lina Shara'an.

Book designed and typeset by Noreen Doyle.
Arabic text typeset by Shatha Abu Aballi and Noreen Doyle.
Arabic book title typography by Mohammed Abu Rayyan.

The United States Embassy in Amman extends its deepest gratitude to the Government of Jordan and the Jordanian people for their steadfast cooperation throughout 75 years of partnership. It is this unwavering support, collaborative spirit, and enduring partnership that have made the achievements in this book possible.

CC BY-NC-ND
Attribution-NonCommercial-NoDerivatives 4.0 International
creativecommons.org/licenses/by-nc-nd/4.0/

Individual photographs are copyrighted by their respective copyright holders.

The American Center of Research
Alexandria, Virginia—Amman, Jordan
acorjordan.org

ISBN: 978-1-955918-19-0

Acknowledgment

All of the projects and efforts represented here have also received support from many other American, Jordanian, and international governments, nonprofit organizations, universities, and private individuals. Too numerous to include in this volume, those contributors are here collectively acknowledged for their significant past and ongoing support of Jordanian cultural heritage.

Only with such cooperation and community could any of the following been achieved.

شكر وتقدير

حظيت جميع المشاريع والجهود المذكورة هنا بدعم العديد من الحكومات الأميركية والأردنية والدولية، بالإضافة إلى المنظمات غير الربحية والجامعات والأفراد. ونظرًا لعددهم الكبير الذي يصعب حصره في هذا المجلد، فإننا نتوجه بالشكر الجماعي لهؤلاء المساهمين لدعمهم الكبير والمستمر للإرث الأثري الأردني.

ولولا هذا التعاون والتعاضد، لما كان من الممكن تحقيق أي من الإنجازات الآتية.

Table of Contents

Foreword by *Chargé de'affaires ad interim* Rohit Nepal vi

The Collaborations
1. Establishing National Parks 2
2. Developing Bethany Beyond the Jordan 3
3. Revealing Roman Petra 4
4. Supporting Petra 5
5. Excavating and Conserving Umm Al-Jimāl 8
6. Fighting Illicit Trafficking of Cultural Heritage 9
7. Surveying Ancient Amman 10
8. Advancing the Roman Aqaba Project 11
9. Establishing the Binational Fulbright Commission 12
10. Endorsing Scholarship and Research 13
11. Mapping Desert Kites 14
12. Studying the Ancient Eastern Deserts 15
13. Establishing the First Digital Database of Sites in the Region 16
14. Creating a National Inventory for Jordan's Heritage 17
15. Improving Tourism Amenities 18
16. Enhancing Access to Mount Nebo 19
17. Providing Access to the Inaccessible 20
18. Diving into Jordan's Maritime Heritage 22
19. Discovering an Islamic Port City 23
20. Preserving Urban Archaeology 24
21. Documenting Early Hashemite Built History 25
22. Discovering the Origins of Art 26
23. Supporting Growth in the Arts 27
24. Conserving Desert Castles 28
25. Understanding Life in the Desert 29
26. Conserving an Umayyad Palace 30
27. Excavating Crusader Castles 30
28. Preserving Petra's Temple of the Winged Lions 32
29. Safeguarding Byzantine Heritage Sites 32
30. Preserving the "Founder's Tomb" in Ancient Capitolias 34
31. Recording Local Traditions for Future Generations 36
32. Preserving Intangible Heritage 37
33. Supporting Foundational Research and Discoveries 38
34. Providing Digital Resources in a Technological Age 38
35. Creating Accessible Tourism 40
36. Supporting Small Businesses 41
37. Highlighting the Medieval Sugar Factory in Ghor as-Safi 42
38. Uncovering History at Tall al-'Umayri 43

جدول المحتويات

مقدمة بقلم القائم بالأعمال روهيت نيبال

معًا من أجل الماضي والحاضر
1. تأسيس المحميّات الوطنية
2. تطوير منطقة المغطس
3. اكتشاف مدينة بترا الرومانية
4. دعم بترا
5. التنقيب عن أم الجمال والمحافظة عليها
6. مكافحة الاتجار غير المشروع بالتراث الثقافي
7. مسح مدينة عمان القديمة
8. تعزيز مشروع العقبة الرومانية
9. تأسيس لجنة فولبرايت الثنائية
10. دعم المنح الدراسية والبحث العلمي
11. خرائط للمصائد الصحراوية
12. دراسة الصحاري الشرقية القديمة
13. تأسيس أول قاعدة بيانات رقمية للمواقع الأثرية في المنطقة
14. إنشاء سجل وطني لتراث الأردن
15. تحسين المرافق السياحية
16. تسهيل الوصول إلى جبل نيبو
17. تسهيل الوصول إلى المواقع العسيرة الوصول
18. الغوص في الإرث البحري الأردني
19. اكتشاف خليج مدينة إسلامية
20. الحفاظ على الآثار الحضرية
21. توثيق المباني المبكرة من العهد الهاشمي
22. اكتشاف أصول الفن
23. دعم ازدهار الفنون
24. حفظ القصور الصحراوية
25. فهم الحياة في الصحراء
26. الحفاظ على قصر أموي
27. التنقيبات الأثرية في قلعة الكرك
28. الحفاظ على معبد الأسود المجنحة في بترا
29. حماية المواقع الأثرية البيزنطية
30. الحفاظ على "قبر المؤسس" في كابيتولياس القديمة
31. توثيق التقاليد المحلية للأجيال القادمة
32. توثيق التراث اللامادي
33. دعم البحث والاكتشافات المؤسسية
34. توفير الموارد الرقمية في العصر الرقمي
35. سياحة متاحة للجميع
36. دعم الشركات الصغيرة وتأسيسها
37. تسليط الضوء على مصنع السكر في غور الصافي من العصور الإسلامية الوسيطة
38. الكشف عن تاريخ تل العُميري

39. Illuminating the "Dark Ages"	44
40. Enhancing Understanding of the Ancient Kingdoms of Jordan	45
41. Excavating Pella, Hub of the Ancient World	45
42. Fostering Intellectual Exchange	48
43. Elevating Standards of Tourism	49
44. Interpreting History through Ceramics	50
45. Preserving the Palace at Iraq al-Amir	51
46. Reassessing History	52
47. Conserving a Temple of Artemis	53
48. Founding a New Natural Heritage Museum	54
49. Maintaining a Public Research Library	55
50. Sustaining Cultural Heritage through Engagement of Local Communities	56
51. Building a Rest House at Pella	58
52. Supporting Ecotourism	58
53. Revitalizing Water Management in Petra	60
54. Conserving the Longest Tunnel of the Classical World	61
55. Developing and Diversifying Tourism Products	62
56. Rebuilding Ancient Monuments	63
57. Conducting Emergency Excavations	64
58. Restoring the Qasr Al-Muwaqqar Reservoir	65
59. Improving the Tourism Experience	66
60. Growing Local Capacity in Rural Jordan	67
61. Revitalizing Madaba	67
62. Building Economic Sustainability through Tourism	70
63. Documenting the History of the Deserts	71
64. Conveying the Stories of the Holy Sites of Jordan	72
65. Expanding Destination Tourism	73
66. Exploring the Unknown	74
67. Saving Ancient History in Urban Environments	75
68. Supporting Significant Publications	76
69. Restoring Religiously Significant Sites	77
70. Exploring Jordan's Southern Reaches	78
71. Strengthening Community Ties to Heritage Sites	79
72. Navigating Ancient Roads and Settlements	80
73. Supporting Research at the Cradle of American Archaeology in Jordan	81
74. Granting Fellowships to Experience Jordan	82
75. Chronicling Rock Art and Epigraphy in Wadi Rum	83
Photo Captions and Credits	86

39. إلقاء الضوء على العصور المظلمة
40. تعزيز فهمنا للممالك القديمة في الأردن
41. التنقيبات الأثرية في بيلا (محطة قوافل العالم القديم)
42. دعم التبادل الفكري
43. رفع معايير السياحة
44. قراءة تاريخ المنطقة من الفخار
45. الحفاظ على القصر في عراق الأمير
46. مراجعة التاريخ
47. الحفاظ على معبد أرتيمس
48. إنشاء متحف جديد للتراث الطبيعي
49. صيانة مكتبة عامة للأبحاث
50. مشروع استدامة الإرث الثقافي بمشاركة المجتمعات المحلية
51. بناء بيت استقبال في بيلا
52. دعم السياحة البيئية
53. إحياء نظام المياه في بترا
54. حماية أطول قناة في العالم الكلاسيكي
55. تعزيز المنتجات السياحية وتنويعها
56. إعادة إحياء المعالم القديمة
57. الحفريات الطارئة
58. ترميم خزّان الموقر الصحراوي
59. تحسين التجربة السياحية
60. تنمية القدرات المحلية في الريف الأردني
61. تطوير مدينة مادبا
62. تحقيق الاستدامة الاقتصادية من خلال السياحة
63. توثيق تاريخ الصحراء
64. سرد قصص المواقع المقدسة في الأردن
65. تعزيز سياحة الوجهات
66. استكشاف المجهول
67. إنقاذ التاريخ القديم في البيئات الحضرية
68. دعم المنشورات المهمة
69. ترميم المواقع ذات الأهمية الدينية
70. استكشاف الجنوب الأردني
71. تعزيز الروابط المجتمعية مع المواقع الأثرية
72. البحث في الطرق والمستقرات القديمة
73. دعم البحث العلمي في مهد علم الآثار الأميركي في الأردن
74. منح زمالات للأردن للتجربة
75. تأريخ الفنون الصخرية والكتابات في وادي رم

وصف الصور والملكية

*Together for Past and Present:
75 Years of Cultural Heritage
Collaboration between the
United States and Jordan*

Foreword by *Chargé d'affaires ad interim* Rohit Nepal

Wandering through Jordan's breathtaking archeological sites, visitors are immersed in the ancient facades, chiseled stones, and rich landscapes that reflect the history, memory, and identity of Jordan. For centuries, American tourists, academics and researchers, businesspeople and diplomats have marveled at these edifices of Jordan's past, learning about the stories and traditions that these sites embody.

One of the earliest American cultural attachés to Jordan, Robert Curran, visited Petra in the early 1960s. He described riding on muleback, staying in a rustic camp, and experiencing a "very special time" in Jordan's Rose City. U.S. diplomats since have done the same, with generations of American ambassadors reminiscing fondly about Jordan's natural beauty, its mesmerizing antiquities, and weekly Friday jaunts to the country's spectacular deserts and remains of the past. During my time in Jordan, like so many Americans before me, I have been truly awestruck by the extraordinary archeological splendors across the country, and by the equally extraordinary Jordanians I've had the privilege of meeting, who cherish and safeguard these treasures.

From the outset of our official bilateral relationship in 1949, the United States government has deeply respected Jordan's heritage, and understood the importance of our partnership in helping preserve Jordan's rich history and unique traditions. Over the years, Americans and Jordanians have worked side by side to discover new artifacts through joint archeological fieldwork, ensure accessibility to renowned archeological sites, and implement educational programs to increase awareness about the importance of Jordan's cultural legacy.

Since 1957, the U.S. government has partnered with Jordan to invest nearly $125 million to help restore, develop, and safeguard its archeological treasures, historic sites, and iconic tourist destinations such as Petra, Al Maghtas (Baptism Site), and Jerash. Our investment has supported an increase in the number of visitors to Jordan, enhanced sustainable tourism, developed local economies through creation of small enterprises and artisanal markets, and created new job opportunities in the tourism sector and in restoration and maintenance of historical landmarks. This book showcases only a small selection of the cooperative work between the United States and Jordan, not a comprehensive summary of all of our partnership efforts to enhance Jordan's cultural heritage sites – to do so would require several more volumes!

This book is more than a record of past successes. It is a testament to a relationship that began under the governance and visionary direction of His Majesty the late King Abdullah I bin Al Hussein, and that continues to this day with His Majesty King Abdullah II ibn Al Hussein. It is a reflection of the partnership that has deepened and strengthened over the course of 15 U.S presidencies and four Jordanian monarchs. And it is a tribute to the ongoing friendship between the American and Jordanian people that began over 75 years ago and continues to flourish and shape a legacy of cooperation for decades to come.

Rohit Nepal
Chargé d'Affaires ad interim

معًا من أجل الماضي والحاضر:
75 عامًا من التعاون في مجال التراث الثقافي بين الولايات المتحدة والأردن

مقدمة بقلم القائم بالأعمال روهيت نيبال

عند التجوّل في المواقع الأثرية الساحرة في الأردن، يجد الزائر نفسه مأسورًا بجمال الواجهات القديمة، والأحجار المنحوتة بعناية، والمناظر الطبيعية الغنية التي تعكس تاريخ الأردن وذاكرته الثقافية وهويته. على مرّ العصور، أبهرت هذه المعالم السياح، والأكاديميين، والباحثين، ورجال الأعمال، والدبلوماسيين الأمريكيين، بما تحمله من عبق ماضي الأردن، حيث اكتشفوا القصص والتقاليد التي ترويها هذه المواقع.

في مطلع الستينيات، زار روبرت كوران، الذي يعد من أوائل الملحقين الثقافيين الأمريكيين في الأردن، مدينة البتراء. وقد تحدث عن تجربته الفريدة بركوب الدواب، والإقامة في مخيم ريفي بسيط، وقضاء "لحظات لا تُنسى" في المدينة الوردية في الأردن. ومنذ ذلك الحين، سار الدبلوماسيون الأمريكيون على النهج نفسه، حيث يتذكر السفراء الأمريكيون الذي تعاقبوا على تلك المهمة، بحنين جمال الطبيعة في الأردن، وآثاره الساحرة، ورحلاتهم خلال عطلة نهاية الأسبوع إلى الصحراء الخلابة وآثارها التاريخية. وخلال مدة إقامتي في الأردن، ذهلتُ، تمامًا مثل العديد من الأمريكيين الذين سبقوني، بروعة المواقع الأثرية المنتشرة في جميع أنحاء المملكة، وحظيت بشرف اللقاء بنخبة مميزة من الأردنيين الذين يعتزون بهذه الكنوز العريقة ويحافظون عليها.

منذ بداية العلاقات الثنائية الرسمية بين البلدين في عام 1949، أظهرت الولايات المتحدة اهتمامًا بالغًا بتراث الأردن، وأدركت أهمية هذه الشراكة في الحفاظ على تاريخ الأردن الغني وتقاليده الفريدة. وعلى مرّ السنين، عمل الأردنيين والأمريكيين بشكل وثيق لاكتشاف قطع أثرية جديدة من خلال أعمال التنقيب المشتركة، وتسهيل الوصول إلى المواقع الأثرية الشهيرة، وتنفيذ برامج تعليمية تهدف إلى تعزيز الوعي بأهمية التراث الثقافي للأردن.

وخلال فترة شراكة الولايات المتحدة مع الأردن منذ عام 1957، استثمرت الحكومة الأمريكية نحو 125 مليون دولار للمساعدة في ترميم وتطوير وحماية الكنوز الأثرية في الأردن ومواقعه التاريخية ووجهاته السياحية الشهيرة مثل البتراء والمغطس وجرش. وقد ساهم ذلك بشكل كبير في زيادة عدد الزوار إلى الأردن، وتعزيز السياحة المستدامة، وتطوير الاقتصادات المحلية من خلال إنشاء المشاريع الصغيرة والأسواق الحرفية، بالإضافة إلى توفير فرص عمل جديدة في قطاع السياحة وترميم وصيانة المواقع الأثرية. يعرض هذا الكتاب جانبًا من أوجه التعاون بين الولايات المتحدة والأردن، ولكنه لا يُعدّ ملخصًا شاملاً لجميع الجهود المبذولة في تعزيز مواقع التراث الثقافي في الأردن، حيث يتطلب توثيق ذلك تأليف العديد من المجلدات الأخرى.

هذا الكتاب ليس مجرد سجل للإنجازات السابقة، بل هو شهادة حية على علاقة راسخة نشأت في عهد الملك الراحل عبد الله الأول بن الحسين، واستمرت حتى يومنا هذا في عهد جلالة الملك عبد الله الثاني ابن الحسين. وهو انعكاس لشراكة بدأت وازدهرت على مدار 15 فترة رئاسة أمريكية وأربعة ملوك أردنيين، ويعبّر عن التقدير العميق للصداقة المستمرة بين الشعبين الأمريكي والأردني، التي بدأت منذ أكثر من 75 عامًا وما زالت مزدهرة، لتشكل إرثًا مشتركًا من التعاون الذي سيستمر لعقود عديدة قادمة.

روهيت نيبال
القائم بالأعمال

Together *for* Past *and* Present

Cultural Heritage Collaborations *between the* **United States** *and* **Jordan** *on the* 75th Anniversary *of* Their Bilateral Relations

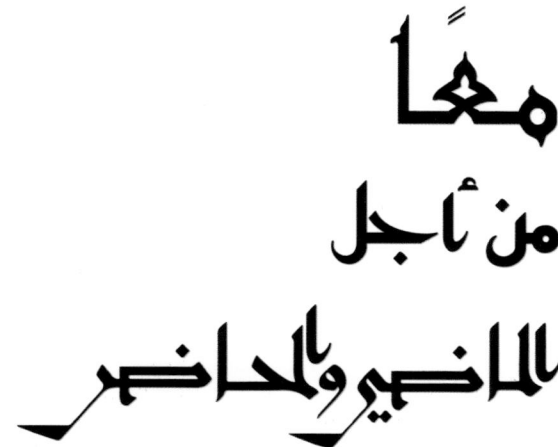

معًا من أجل الماضي والحاضر

أوجه التعاون
في إحياء الإرث الثقافي
بين
الولايات المتحدة الأميركية
و المملكة الأردنية الهاشمية
بمناسبة
الذكرى الخامسة والسبعين
لإرساء
العلاقات الثنائية المتبادلة

Establishing National Parks

تأسيس المحميات الوطنية

Jordan maintains its cultural heritage through a network of beautiful national parks and archaeological preserves, which are the oldest in the region. Collaboration with Jordan on these efforts began in the 1950s, with Point Four technical assistance funding (announced by the late U.S. President Truman) and the expertise of the U.S. National Park Service (NPS), supporting the repair of monuments and creation of parks. In 1965, twelve NPS employees and their families moved to Jordan, where for two years they helped develop a master plan for Petra (shown here), a site designated as one of Jordan's first national parks and famously home to the ancient Nabataean civilization. Jordan's park system has continued to grow, often with U.S. partnership, to protect thousands of archaeological sites and ten nature reserves spanning nearly 2,000 square miles.

يحافظ الأردن على تراثه الثقافي من خلال شبكة من المحميات الوطنية الجميلة والمحميات الأثرية، والتي تُعد من الأقدم في المنطقة. بدأ هذا التعاون مع الأردن في خمسينات القرن الماضي بتمويل من برنامج (Point Four) - الذي أعلنه الرئيس الأمريكي الراحل ترومان- وبخبرات دائرة المحميات الوطنية الأميركية التي دعمت ترميم المعالم الأثرية وإنشاء المحميات. وفي عام 1965، انتقل اثنا عشر موظفًا من دائرة المتنزهات الوطنية وعائلاتهم إلى الأردن، حيث ساعدوا لمدة عامين في تطوير خطة شاملة لبترا التي تظهر في الصورة، والتي صُنفت كواحدة من أولى المحميات الوطنية في الأردن وموطن حضارة الأنباط القديمة الشهيرة. واستمر نظام المحميات في الأردن في النمو - غالبًا بالشراكة مع الولايات المتحدة الأميركية- لحماية آلاف المواقع الأثرية وعشر محميات طبيعية تمتد على مساحة ما يقارب من 2000 ميل مربع.

Developing Bethany Beyond the Jordan

تطوير منطقة المغطس

Nestled along the serene banks of the Jordan River a few miles north of the Dead Sea, the Bethany Beyond the Jordan site is dotted with ancient ruins, including churches and baptismal pools that bear testament to the site's enduring significance. In 2006, USAID funded the development of the Baptism Site Business Plan, which outlined the strategic development and promotion of the site, emphasizing its potential to become a major faith-based tourism anchor, second only to Jerusalem/Bethlehem in Christian religious importance. Since 2006, Bethany Beyond the Jordan—the place where John is believed to have baptized Jesus—has seen major growth in tourism, with hundreds of thousands of visitors annually.

على ضفاف نهر الأردن الهادئة وعلى بُعد بضعة أميال من شمال البحر الميت، يقع موقع "بيت عنيا" الذي يزخر ببقايا أثرية قديمة، بما في ذلك الكنائس وأحواض المعمودية التي تشهد على الأهمية الدائمة للموقع. في عام 2006، مولت الوكالة الأميركية للتنمية الدولية تطوير خطة الأعمال لموقع المغطس، والتي وضعت استراتيجية لتطوير الموقع والترويج له، مؤكدة أنه مؤهل ليصبح مركزًا رئيسًا للسياحة الدينية، إذ إنه يأتي في المنزلة الثانية بعد القدس وبيت لحم من حيث الأهمية الدينية عند المسيحيين. وشهد الموقع منذ عام 2006 زيادة كبيرة في عدد السائحين؛ إذ يستقبل مئات الآلاف من الزوار سنويًا، والذين يعتقدون أن هذا هو المكان الذي ي عمَّد يوحنا المعمدان فيه السيد المسيح.

Revealing Roman Petra

اكتشاف مدينة بترا الرومانية

Deep within the winding red sandstone canyons and cliffs of the ancient city of Petra, financial support from USAID from 1997 to 1999 helped reveal its Roman history. Petra famously represents the apex of the Nabataean people, who, after thriving independently for centuries, were the last holdouts in the region against the Roman Empire. The work supported by USAID allowed the excavation of the colonnaded central street that welcomes tourists today and revealed a series of shops or taverns and a stairway leading to the upper market, improving understanding of Petra's urban history.

في أعماق الممرات المتعرجة والمنحدرات الحمراء ذات الحجر الرملي في مدينة بترا القديمة، ساهم الدعم المالي المقدَّم من الوكالة الأميركية للتنمية الدولية بين عامي 1997 و1999 في الكشف على تاريخ بترا الروماني. وتُعد بترا رمزًا لحضارة الأنباط، الذين ازدهروا لقرون عديدة مستقلين بأنفسهم، فكانوا آخر المعاقل في المنطقة التي صمدت أمام الإمبراطورية الرومانية. ومكّن الدعم المقدم من الوكالة من التنقيب عن الشارع الرئيس المعمَّد الذي يرحب بالزوار اليوم، ومن الكشف عن سلسلة من المحال أو الأنزال، وعن درج يؤدي إلى السوق العلوية، فعززت هذه الاكتشافات فهمنا لتاريخ بترا الحضري.

Supporting Petra

(and following pages)

With more than a million people visiting the site annually, the ancient Nabataean city of Petra and its splendid rock-cut temples and tombs have left an indelible mark on world heritage. In 1968, the U.S. National Park Service supported the creation of Petra's first master plan, focused on site preservation and managing tourism growth. The plan identified mitigating flooding at the city's winding canyon entrance, known as the Siq, as the foremost priority. USAID subsequently supported replication of the ancient dams that had served that same purpose in antiquity. In 1994, USAID financed a second master plan, recommending improvements to the visitor center, trail identification, landscaping, and signage. In August 2024, U.S. Ambassador Yael Lempert announced a $15 million grant to Petra to support green growth initiatives in the park.

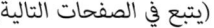

دعم بترا

(يتبع في الصفحات التالية)

يزور أكثر من مليون شخص سنويًا مدينة بترا النبطية القديمة بمعابدها ومقابرها المنحوتة في الصخر، والتي تركت بصمة لا تُنسى على التراث العالمي. وفي عام 1968، دعمت دائرة المحميات الوطنية الأميركية إعداد أول خطة شاملة لبترا، ركزت على الحفاظ على الموقع وإدارة النمو السياحي فيه، وجعلت الخطة مواجهة الفيضانات التي تهدد مدخل الوادي المتعرج المعروف باسم السيق أولويتها الأولى. واستمرت الوكالة الأميركية للتنمية الدولية في المساعدة على إعادة بناء السدود القديمة التي كانت تؤدي الغرض نفسه في العصور القديمة. وفي عام 1994، مولت الوكالة إعداد خطة شاملة ثانية، أوصت بتحسين مركز الزوار، وبتحديد المسارات السياحية، وبتنسيق المشهد الطبيعي، وبوضع اللوحات الإرشادية. وفي آب 2024، أعلنت السفيرة الأميركية يائيل لمبرت عن منحة بقيمة 15 مليون دولار لدعم مبادرات النمو الأخضر في محمية بترا.

Excavating and Conserving Umm Al-Jimāl

The Princeton Expedition undertook a survey of Umm Al-Jimāl in 1904–1905 and in 1909. Some six decades later, Calvin College (Grand Rapids, Michigan) started work at the site that has continued into the current century. From 2012 to 2014, the U.S. Department of State's Ambassador's Fund for Cultural Preservation supported excavation and conservation of the House XVII–XVIII complex. Jordanian experts carried out the conservation work, while a Jordanian-American team conducted the excavation. Umm Al-Jimāl, particularly House XVII–XVIII, is the best-preserved evidence of the traditions and practices of the Hauran (a region in northern Jordan and southern Syria), which have persisted over millennia. These joint Jordanian-American efforts directly contributed to Umm Al-Jimāl being inscribed as a UNESCO World Heritage Site in 2024.

التنقيب عن أم الجمال والمحافظة عليها

قامت بعثة جامعة برينستون في عامي 1904-1905 و1909 بمسح أثري لموقع أم الجمال. وبعد نحو ستة عقود، بدأت كلية كالفن (غراند رابيدز، ميشغان) العمل في الموقع، والذي ما يزال مستمرًا حتى العقد الحالي. وفي الفترة من 2012 إلى 2014، دعم صندوق السفراء للحفاظ على التراث الثقافي مشروعًا للتنقيب والحفاظ الأثريين في أم الجمال، وتحديدًا في مجمع البيت السابع عشر-الثامن عشر، فنفذ خبراء أردنيون أعمال الحفاظ، بينما أجرى فريق أردني أميركي أعمال التنقيب. وتُعد أم الجمال، والبيت السابع عشر-الثامن عشر خاصة، خير شاهد وصل إلينا على أنماط الحياة في منطقة حوران، والتي دامت آلاف السنين. وساهمت هذه الجهود الأردنية الأميركية بشكل مباشر في إدراج موقع أم الجمال على قائمة اليونسكو لمواقع التراث العالمي في عام 2024.

Fighting Illicit Trafficking of Cultural Heritage

In cooperation with the Government of Jordan, the U.S. Embassy in Amman sponsored training for fifty Jordanian cultural heritage experts, museum staff, and law-enforcement officials. The training focused on measures to safeguard Jordan's cultural artifacts from looting, illicit trafficking, and exploitation in support of the U.S.-Jordan Cultural Property Agreement, initially signed in 2019, to help combat the illegal trade in antiquities that threatens Jordan's cultural treasures. This agreement—along with joint efforts to further enhance information sharing, expand prevention measures, and strengthen legal frameworks to investigate cultural property crime—directly contributed to the return in 2022 of nine illicitly trafficked Jordanian artifacts from the United States, including the two seen here.

Surveying Ancient Amman

مسح مدينة عمان القديمة

Humanity has called the hills and ridges of Amman home for at least 9,000 years, making it one of the longest continuously inhabited places in the world. In 1988, USAID sponsored a comprehensive archaeological survey of the greater Amman area, revealing even more about this bastion of civilizations. The project collected archaeological data on successive settlement systems in the region of ancient Ammon/Philadelphia (modern Amman), and it created an inventory of sites. The project ultimately promoted the preservation of cultural property concurrent with the planned economic development of the modern Jordanian capital, ensuring the preservation across a long arc of human heritage.

سكنت البشرية التلال والمرتفعات في عمان منذ ما لا يقل عن 9000 عام، ما يجعلها واحدة من أقدم المدن المأهولة بشكل مستمر في العالم. وفي عام 1988، دعمت الوكالة الأميركية للتنمية الدولية مسحًا أثريًا شاملًا لمنطقة عمان الكبرى، كشف عن المزيد من حضارة المدينة. واستهدف المشروع جمع بيانات أثرية عن أنظمة الاستقرار المتعاقبة في منطقة عمُّون/فيلادلفيا القديمة (عمان الحديثة)، بالإضافة إلى تحديد المواقع الأثرية الواقعة في نطاق المدينة. وساهم المشروع في الحفاظ على الممتلكات الثقافية للعاصمة الأردنية الحديثة في سياق التنمية الاقتصادية المنوي تنفيذها هناك، ما ضمن الحفاظ على هذا الإرث الإنساني الممتد عبر التاريخ.

10

Advancing the Roman Aqaba Project

تعزيز مشروع العقبة الرومانية

The southernmost point of Jordan extends to the sunny waters of the Red Sea at the Gulf of Aqaba. For thousands of years, people of the region have accessed the maritime world from this point. From 1994 to 2002 the U.S. National Endowment for the Humanities and USAID supported a collaborative effort to incorporate archaeological and environmental surveys, excavations, and analyses of material remains of the ancient city of Ayla (modern Aqaba). Multiple field seasons yielded a comprehensive understanding of the city's historical phases from the Nabataean, Roman, Byzantine, and early Islamic periods. Notable archaeological findings included the discovery of the world's earliest known purpose-built Christian church, portions of the Byzantine city wall, and a wealth of artifacts that shed light on trade and daily life in the ancient city.

تمتد أقصى نقطة في جنوب الأردن حتى تصل مياه البحر الأحمر المشمسة في خليج العقبة. وعلى مدى آلاف السنين، وصل الناس من هذا الموقع إلى عالم البحار. وبين عامي 1994 و2002، دعم الصندوق الوطني للعلوم الإنسانية والوكالة الأميركية للتنمية الدولية جهدًا تعاونيًا شمل مسوحات أثرية وبيئية، وتنقيبات، وتحليلًا للبقايا المادية للمدينة القديمة أيلة (العقبة الحديثة). وأسفرت عدة مواسم تنقيب ميدانية عن فهم شامل للمراحل التاريخية للمدينة منذ الفترات النبطية، والرومانية، والبيزنطية، والإسلامية المبكرة. ومن بين الاكتشافات الأثرية البارزة، عُثر على أقدم كنيسة معروفة في العالم، وعلى أجزاء من سور المدينة البيزنطي، وعلى مجموعة وفيرة من القطع الأثرية التي تسلط الضوء على التجارة والحياة اليومية في المدينة القديمة.

11

Establishing the Binational Fulbright Commission

تأسيس لجنة فولبرايت الثنائية

Established in May 1993, the Binational Fulbright Commission in Jordan receives funding from the Hashemite Kingdom of Jordan and the United States of America. The commission inaugurated its offices in Amman, known as the Fulbright House, on December 8, 1994, in the presence of HRH Prince El Hassan bin Talal (pictured here). The Fulbright Program aims to foster mutual understanding between the people of the United States and Jordan by providing grants and fellowships to students, teachers, and scholars for study, teaching, lecturing, and cross-cultural research in the United States and Jordan.

تأسست لجنة فولبرايت الثنائية في الأردن في أيار من عام 1993، وهي تتلقى تمويلًا من المملكة الأردنية الهاشمية ومن الولايات المتحدة الأميركية. افتتحت اللجنة مكاتبها في عمان، المعروفة ببيت فولبرايت، في 8 كانون الأول 1994 بحضور صاحب السمو الملكي الأمير الحسن ابن طلال (الذي يظهر في الصورة). ويهدف برنامج فولبرايت إلى تعزيز الفهم المتبادل بين شعبي الولايات المتحدة والأردن من خلال توفير المنح الدراسية والزمالات للطلاب والمعلمين، والعلماء للدراسة، والتعليم، والمحاضرة، وإجراء البحوث في ثقافات الولايات المتحدة والأردن.

12

Endorsing Scholarship and Research

Since 1994, the Binational Fulbright Commission in Jordan has awarded fellowships to 811 Jordanians and 894 Americans. In 2024, the fellow seen here conducted a photographic research project, replicating 100-year-old photographs throughout Petra. Photographers duplicated the location, angle, height, and perspective of the historic images using a field tablet linked to a camera. These photos will be published in an upcoming book tentatively titled "Petra Rephotographed: A Century of Change in the Rose Red City," which is scheduled for release in the fall of 2025—100 years after the original historic photographs were published.

دعم المنح الدراسية والبحث العلمي

منذ عام 1994، منحت لجنة فولبرايت الثنائية في الأردن زمالات لـ 811 أردنيًا و894 أميركيًا. وفي عام 2024، نفَّذ الزميل الظاهر في الصورة مشروع بحث فوتوغرافي، أعاد فيه تصوير صور فوتوغرافية عمرها 100 عام التُقطت في جميع أنحاء بترا. وأعاد المصورون تصوير المواقع، والزوايا، والارتفاعات، والمناظير للصور التاريخية باستخدام جهاز لوحي ميداني متصل بآلة تصوير. وستُنشر هذه الصور في كتاب قيد التحضير بعنوان مبدئي هو: "بترا: إعادة تصويرها - قرن من التغيير في المدينة الوردية"، من المقرر أن يصدر في خريف 2025، أي بعد 100 عام من نشر الصور التاريخية الأصلية.

13

Mapping Desert Kites

خرائط للمصائد الصحراوية

The expansive eastern deserts of Jordan hide untold secrets of which scholars have unveiled only a small portion. In 2022, the U.S. National Science Foundation funded a project designed to study the prehistoric phenomenon of "desert kites" (stone-built animal traps) stretching across the eastern desert of Jordan. International collaborators combined high-resolution drone mapping with survey and excavation data to understand the construction, use, and context in which these thousands of traps operated. Sitting on and near the surface today, these kites are only one of the many mysteries the deserts still hold.

تخفي الصحاري الشرقية الفسيحة في الأردن أسرارًا، لم يكشف العلماء سوى عن جزء يسير منها. وفي عام 2022، مولت مؤسسة العلوم الوطنية مشروعًا لدراسة ظاهرة "المصائد الصحراوية" (مصائد حجرية لصيد الحيوانات)، والتي تنتشر في الصحراء الشرقية الأردن وتعود إلى عصور ما قبل التاريخ. وتعاون الباحثون الدوليون في دمج نتائج المسح الجوي باستخدام الطائرات بدون طيار العالية الدقة بنتائج المسوحات والتنقيبات الأثرية لفهم طريقة بناء هذه المصائد، وطرق استخدامها، والسياق الذي عملت فيه الآلاف منها. وعلى الرغم من أنها تقع اليوم على سطح الأرض أو بالقرب منه، إلا أن هذه المصائد الصحراوية ليست سوى واحد من الألغاز العديدة التي ما تزال الصحاري تشتمل عليها.

Studying the Ancient Eastern Deserts

دراسة الصحراء الشرقية القديمة

Supported by U.S. Department of State-funded fellowships (2002, 2010, 2013, 2023) and by the U.S. National Endowment for the Humanities (2018), surveys and excavations in Wadi al-Qattafi and at Wisad Pools in Jordan's panhandle east of Azraq have significantly increased the collective knowledge of these areas and their long history. These sites are located in the eastern desert of Jordan in the "Badia" (Badlands) along the edge of the Black Desert, just north of the Saudi Arabian border, in what today appears an inhospitable environment but was not always so. During the Neolithic era (approximately 8500 to 5000 BCE), the landscape sustained hunting, herding, and trapping. Numerous newly discovered structures have shed light on how the deserts of today looked millennia ago as more lush environments.

بدعم من زمالات ممولة من وزارة الخارجية الأميركية في الأعوام (2002، 2010، 2013، 2023) والصندوق الوطني للعلوم الإنسانية (2018)، ساهمت مجموعة من المسوحات والتنقيبات في وادي القطافي وفي برك الوساد في الزاوية الشرقية للأردن، شرقي الأزرق، في زيادة معرفتنا بهذه المناطق وبتاريخها الطويل زيادة كبيرة. وتقع هذه المواقع في الصحراء الشرقية للأردن في منطقة "البادية" على حافة الحَرَّة، شمالي الحدود السعودية، في بيئة تبدو اليوم غير صالحة للسكن، ولكنها لم تكن دائمًا على هذا النحو، فخلال العصر الحجري الحديث (حوالي 8500 إلى 5000 قبل الميلاد)، كانت البيئة مناسبة للصيد، والرعي، ولإقامة المصائد. وأظهر العدد الكبير من المنشآت المكتشفة حديثًا أن الصحاري الحالية كانت قبل آلاف السنين بيئات أكثر خصبًا.

15

Establishing the First Digital Database of Sites in the Region

تأسيس أول قاعدة بيانات رقمية للمواقع الأثرية في المنطقة

The diverse heritage sites of Jordan offer a veritable cornucopia of time and cultures. Protecting and preserving such vibrant and diverse places begins with identifying and enumerating them. In 1990, USAID supported the creation of the Jordan Antiquities Database and Information System (JADIS). The first of its kind in the Arab world, JADIS was instrumental in cataloging 10,840 archaeological sites in Jordan. After a remarkable 15 years of operation, the database was superseded by a new iteration, MEGA-Jordan, which today holds records of 15,180 sites.

تشتمل المواقع الأثرية المتنوعة في الأردن على مجموعة متنوعة من العصور والثقافات، لذا، تبدأ حماية هذه المواقع النابضة بالحياة والمتنوعة والحفاظ عليها من خلال تحديدها وحصرها. وفي عام 1990، مولت الوكالة الأمريكية للتنمية الدولية إنشاء قاعدة بيانات لنظام الآثار الأردن (JADIS)، كانت الأولى من نوعها في العالم العربي، ولعبت دورًا أساسيًا في فهرسة أكثر من 10,840 موقعًا أثريًا في الأردن. وبعد 15 عامًا من العمل، استُبدلت بنسخة جديدة تُدعى MEGA-Jordan تحتوي اليوم على سجلات لأكثر من 15,180 موقعًا.

16

Creating a National Inventory for Jordan's Heritage

إنشاء سجل وطني لتراث الأردن

Objects, whether everyday utensils or significant works of art, tell tales of their time, and it is the work of archaeologists to extract from them stories of the past. Since 2022, the U.S. Department of State has funded a collaboration led by Jordan's Department of Antiquities to establish a single national inventory system for Jordan's movable cultural heritage. The effort has streamlined the cataloging and maintenance of invaluable historical and archaeological assets and the stories that they hold, thereby ensuring their protection for generations to come. The inventory includes the votive stone slab shown here, representing the presence of a deity from Petra. Donated by a man named Hayyan, son of Nybat, this object is thought to represent one of the consorts of the Nabataean god Dushara, perhaps either al-'Uzza or Allat, who are equated with Egyptian Isis and Aphrodite/Venus of the Hellenistic and Roman pantheons.

تحكي البقايا الأثرية، سواء كانت أدوات يومية أو أعمالًا فنية مهمة، قصصًا عن زمانها، فيعمل علماء الآثار على استخراج حكايات الماضي منها. ومنذ عام 2022، مولت وزارة الخارجية الأميركية مشروعًا تعاونيًّا، تقوده دائرة الآثار العامة لإنشاء نظام سجل وطني واحد للتراث الثقافي المنقول في الأردن. ويسهِّل هذا الجهد فهرسة وصيانة الموارد التاريخية والأثرية الثمينة والقصص التي تحملها، لضمان حفظها للأجيال القادمة. في هذه الصورة ترى نصبًا نذوريًّا لإله من بترا، قدَّمه رجل يدعى حيان بن نيبات، يُعتقد أنه يمثل إلهة من زوجات الإله النبطي ذو الشرى، إما العُزى أو اللات اللتان تماثلان الإلهة المصرية إيزيس وإلهة الحب والجمال الإغريقية/الرومانية أفروديت/فينوس.

17

Improving Tourism Amenities

تحسين المرافق السياحية

Less than an hour north of Amman, the expansive ancient city of Jerash, inhabited for more than 6,000 years, is one of the most impressive sites in the region. Renowned today as perhaps the best-preserved provincial Roman city, it once had more than a thousand columns, dozens of which remain standing today. In the 1960s, USAID supported construction of the original tourist rest house—one of several U.S.-Jordanian partnerships over the years to develop the site for tourism. Today, Jerash is one of the most-visited sites in Jordan, welcoming hundreds of thousands of visitors annually.

تقع مدينة جرش القديمة الفسيحة على بُعد أقل من ساعة شمالي عمان، وقد سكنها الناس لأكثر من 6000 سنة، فهي واحدة من أبرز المواقع في تلك المنطقة. ولعل جرش اليوم أفضل مدينة رومانية محفوظة من مدن الولايات الرومانية، كان فيها يومًا أكثر من ألف عمود، لا يزال العديد منها قائمًا اليوم. وكان دعم الوكالة الأميركية للتنمية الدولية في الستينات لبناء استراحة سياحية تقليدية واحدة من الشراكات العديدة التي عُقدت على مر السنين لتطوير السياحة في الموقع. واليوم، تُعد جرش واحدة من أكثر المواقع زيارة في الأردن، إذ تستقبل مئات الآلاف من السائحين سنويًّا.

18

Enhancing Access to Mount Nebo

تسهيل الوصول إلى جبل نيبو

Rising thousands of feet above the Jordan Valley and overlooking the Dead Sea, Mount Nebo is regarded by many as the place from which Moses viewed the Promised Land before his death. In the 1960s, USAID funded the construction of the first paved road to this site, connecting the ancient site of Mount Nebo to the surrounding area. It is now less than a one-hour drive from Amman, making Mount Nebo more accessible to tourists and visitors. As a result, nearly 500,000 people visit the site every year.

يرتفع جبل نيبو آلاف الأقدام فوق وادي الأردن، مُطلًّا على البحر الميت. ويعده كثيرون المكان الذي شاهد منه النبي موسى أرض الميعاد قبل وفاته. وفي الستينات، مولت الوكالة الأميركية للتنمية الدولية شق أول طريق معبد إلى هذا الموقع، وصل الموقعَ القديم لجبل نيبو بالمنطقة المحيطة به، فلم يعد يبعد أكثر من ساعة بالسيارة من عمان - ما جعله أيسر وصولًا للسياح والزوار؛ فيزوره اليوم حوالي 500,000 شخص سنويًا.

Providing Access to the Inaccessible

The stunning desert landscapes sweeping across the dunes and jagged rocky outcrops of Wadi Rum in the south of Jordan are like nowhere else on earth. For most of the last century, when Hollywood movies have needed a setting "out of this world," they have often looked to Wadi Rum. Dozens of movies have been filmed there, including *Lawrence of Arabia* (1962), *The Martian* (2015), *Dune* (2021), and parts of the *Star Wars* film franchise. In the 1960s, USAID supported the construction of the first paved road to Wadi Rum, enhancing access to it and inspiring imagination. This new accessibility boosted tourism in Wadi Rum, allowing for development of various tourist activities such as Jeep safaris, rock climbing, visits to ancient temples and archaeological sites, and overnight stays in Bedouin camps.

تسهيل الوصول إلى المواقع العسيرة الوصول

تتسم المشاهد الصحراوية المدهشة التي تمتد عبر الكثبان الرملية والتكوينات الصخرية الوعرة في وادي رم في جنوب الأردن بجمال لا مثيل له على وجه الأرض. وعلى مدار معظم القرن الماضي، وعندما كان مخرجو أفلام هوليوود يبحثون عن موقع "من خارج هذا العالم"، كانوا كثيرًا ما يستعينون بوادي رم، فصُوِّرت العشرات من الأفلام هناك، بما في ذلك أفلام "لورانس العرب" (1962)، و"المريخي" (2015)، و"الكثيب" (2021)، وأجزاء من سلسلة أفلام "حرب النجوم". وفي الستينات، مولت الوكالة الأميركية للتنمية الدولية شق أول طريق معبد يصل إلى وادي رم، ما سهل الوصول إليه وفتح المجال لخيالنا الجماعي. وعززت هذه الطريق الجديدة السياحة في وادي رم، فتطور العديد من الأنشطة السياحية، مثل رحلات السفاري بسيارات الدفع الرباعي، وتسلق الصخور، وزيارة معابده ومواقعه الأثرية القديمة، والمبيت في المخيمات البدوية.

Diving into Jordan's Maritime Heritage

الغوص في الإرث البحري الأردني

The tranquil coastline of the Gulf of Aqaba has long served as a gateway to Jordan's interior and points farther afield. Aqaba itself has been known as a safe harbor and economic zone for thousands of years, since at least as early as the pharaonic era of ancient Egypt. Yet nearly all of Jordan's underwater mysteries remain unknown. From 2017 to 2018, USAID supported the Royal Marine Conservation Society of Jordan (JREDS) to conduct the first underwater archaeological survey, recovering artifacts, revealing new information about Aqaba's long history, and identifying potential threats to Jordan's maritime heritage. An interactive site map and interpretive panels were also added along the shore to enhance visitor understanding of the historical significance of the site. The city of Aqaba as it is known today was likely founded by the Nabataeans in about 30 BCE, and it thrived with contacts to Petra, Gaza, Egypt, and elsewhere throughout the region by both land and sea. The city prospered under Roman and later Muslim rule with changes through time in international trade routes, as well as in local agriculture and industries. It remains to this day Jordan's only seaport.

لطالما كانت سواحل خليج العقبة الهادئة بمثابة بوابة تفضي إلى الأردن وإلى ما بعده من أماكن. وظلت مدينة العقبة ميناءً آمنًا ومنطقة اقتصادية لآلاف السنين، منذ العصر الفرعوني في مصر القديمة، على الأقل. ومع ذلك، لا تزال معظم أسرارها تحت الماء مجهولة إلى اليوم. ومن 2017 إلى 2018، دعمت الوكالة الأميركية للتنمية الدولية الجمعيةَ الملكية لحماية البيئة البحرية في الأردن في إجراء أول مسح أثري تحت الماء، كشف عن قطع أثرية ومعلومات جديدة عن تاريخ العقبة المديد، بالإضافة إلى أنه حدد التهديدات المحتملة لتراث الأردن البحري. كما وُضعت خريطة تفاعلية للموقع ولوحات تفسيرية على الشاطئ لتعزيز فهم الزوار لأهميته التاريخية. ونقدِّر أن الأنباط قد أسسوا مدينة العقبة، كما نعرفها اليوم، حوالي عام 30 قبل الميلاد، وازدهرت من خلال اتصالاتها عبر البر والبحر ببترا، وغزة، ومصر، وأماكن أخرى في المنطقة. وازدهرت المدينة في أثناء الحكم الروماني، ولاحقًا في أثناء الحكم الإسلامي، وإن أصابت طرق التجارة الدولية بعض التغيرات عبر الزمن، كما تغيرت الزراعة المحلية والصناعات. ولا تزال العقبة إلى يومنا هذا الميناء البحري الوحيد في الأردن.

Discovering an Islamic Port City

اكتشاف خليج مدينة إسلامية

The picturesque port city of Ayla served as one of the most important trade hubs of the early Muslim world. Ayla, in what is today modern Aqaba, was the first Islamic city established outside of Arabia, in the area of an ancient port dating back to Nabataean and Roman times. From 1986 to 1993, as well as in 2018 and 2019, USAID funding supported excavation, interpretation, and public display of Ayla's remains. The excavations offered significant insights into its architectural features, uncovering residential areas, an early mosque, and a network of streets with shops, thus highlighting the city's role as a crucial trading center in the early Islamic period. Discoveries of pottery, coins, and inscriptions provided critical information about daily life, trade activities, and cultural influences in Ayla during its peak as a maritime trading hub.

مدينة أيلة الخلابة، الواقعة اليوم ضمن مدينة العقبة الحديثة، كانت واحدة من أهم مراكز التجارة في العالم الإسلامي المبكر، وهي أول مدينة إسلامية تُؤسس خارج جزيرة العرب، وتقع في منطقة ميناء قديم يعود إلى العصور النبطية والرومانية. ومن عام 1986 إلى 1993، وكذلك في عامَي 2018 و2019، دعم تمويل الوكالة الأميركية للتنمية الدولية أعمال التنقيب، والتفسير، والعرض في الموقع. وكشفت التنقيبات عن جوانب مهمة من ملامحها المعمارية، فقد اكتُشفت مناطق سكنية، ومسجد قديم، وشبكة من الشوارع مع محال تجارية، ما أبرز دور المدينة كمركز تجاري حيوي في الفترة الإسلامية المبكرة. وقدمت اكتشافات الفخار، والنقود، والنقوش معلومات مهمة عن الحياة اليومية في المدينة، وعن أنشطة التجارة، والتأثيرات الثقافية في أيلة خلال ذروتها كمركز تجاري بحري.

Preserving Urban Archaeology

الحفاظ على الآثار الحضرية

The 2nd-century CE Roman Nymphaeum in the heart of downtown Amman stands as a tribute to the grandeur of Roman architectural ingenuity. Once a lavish public fountain adorned with intricate statues and flowing water, this monumental structure served as both a functional water source and a symbol of civic pride in the ancient city. Through careful restoration, a project funded by the U.S. Department of State's Ambassador's Fund for Cultural Preservation from 2014 to 2018 helped safeguard the monument and revive the Nymphaeum's striking features, such as its graceful arches and ornate reliefs. Subsequent site management and rehabilitation plans enhanced the site as a tourism destination, creating a new attraction in downtown Amman. The project served as a case study for management practices for the revival of urban heritage, focusing on sustainable preservation methods.

يُعد سبيل الحوريات الروماني في عمان الراجع إلى القرن الثاني الميلادي شاهدًا على عظمة الإبداع المعماري الروماني. وكان هذا السبيل في السابق نافورة عامة فاخرة مزينة بتماثيل كثيرة التفاصيل تستمد ماءها من مياه جارية، وشكل السبيل في المدينة القديمة مصدرًا للمياه، من جهة، ورمزًا للفخر المدني من جهة أخرى. ومن خلال الترميم الدقيق، ساعد مشروع ممول من صندوق السفراء الأميركي لحفظ التراث الثقافي من عام 2014 إلى عام 2018 في حماية هذا المعلم التذكاري وفي إحياء سماته المذهلة، مثل أقواسه الرشيقة ونقوشه المزخرفة. وعززت خطط إدارة الموقع وإعادة تأهيله اللاحقة سبيل الحوريات كوجهة سياحية، ما أدى إلى إنشاء معلم جذب جديد في وسط مدينة عمان. وكان المشروع بمثابة حالة دراسية لممارسات إحياء التراث الحضري، مع التركيز على أساليب الحفظ المستدام.

Documenting Early Hashemite Built History

توثيق المباني المبكرة من العهد الهاشمي

The built heritage from the early era of Hashemite Jordan is distinct and beautiful. Across Jordan, one can find many wonderfully preserved and accessible historic structures of the last century. In 1997, USAID supported production of *Old Houses of Jordan*, a book that serves as both an introduction and a practical field guide to the architectural features of Jordan's houses built between 1920 and 1950. The book primarily focused on structures in Amman, providing insights into the typical characteristics and reliefs of the region's architecture and preserving a critical record of early Hashemite history.

يتميز التراث المعماري من العهد الهاشمي المبكر بالأردن بالفرادة والجمال. ففي جميع أنحاء الأردن، ترى مباني تاريخية عديدة، بُنيت في القرن الماضي، وما تزال محفوظة في شكل رائع، ويسهل على الناس الوصول إليها. وفي عام 1997، دعمت الوكالة الأمريكية للتنمية الدولية إنتاج كتاب "المنازل القديمة في الأردن"، والذي يُعد مقدمة ودليلًا ميدانيًا عمليًا للسمات المعمارية لبيوت الأردن التي بُنيت بين عامي 1920 و1950. وركز الكتاب، في المقام الأول، على المباني في عمان، حيث قدم رؤى حول الخصائص النموذجية للهندسة المعمارية في المنطقة، وحافظ على سجل بالغ الأهمية للتاريخ الهاشمي المبكر.

Discovering the Origins of Art

Artistic expression is fundamental to and has perhaps defined the human condition since our earliest days. The world-famous 'Ain Ghazal statues, unearthed in Amman, mark a major advancement in human culture. Dating from the Neolithic period, around 7000 BCE, these 15 statues and 15 busts represent some of the earliest-known, large-scale human figures, several of which are or have been on display in the Jordan Museum in Amman, the Smithsonian Institution in Washington, D.C., the British Museum in London, the Louvre Museum in Paris, and the Louvre-Abu Dhabi. This discovery was made possible in 1982, when the United States Information Agency supported the archaeological excavations that uncovered them. Further support of joint Jordanian and American efforts came from the U.S. National Endowment for the Humanities (1988, 1999, 2007, 2017, and 2025), USAID (1993, 2019), and others, to improve understanding of these remarkable finds.

اكتشاف أصول الفن

يُعد التعبير الفني أمرًا أساسيًا للإنسان، بل ربما ميّز الإنسان من سواه منذ أيامه الأولى. وتمثل تماثيل عين غزال الشهيرة، والتي اكتُشفت بعمان، تقدمًا كبيرًا في الثقافة البشرية. تعود هذه التماثيل إلى العصر الحجري الحديث، أي إلى حوالي عام 7000 عام قبل الميلاد، وتشمل 15 تمثالًا و15 تمثالًا نصفيًا، تمثل بعضًا من أقدم التماثيل البشرية الكبيرة المعروفة، والعديد منها معروض حاليًا، أو كان معروضًا، في متحف الأردن بعمان، ومتحف سميثسونيان في واشنطن، والمتحف البريطاني في لندن، ومتحف اللوفر في باريس، ولوفر أبوظبي. اكتُشفت هذه التماثيل عام 1982، عندما دعمت الوكالة الأميركية للمعلومات التنقيبات الأثرية التي كشفت عنها. كما جاء المزيد من الدعم للجهود الأردنية الأميركية المشتركة في عين غزال من الصندوق الوطني للعلوم الإنسانية في الأعوام (1988، 1999، 2007، 2017، 2025)، ومن الوكالة الأميركية للتنمية الدولية في عامَي (1993، 2019) ومن جهات أخرى، ما زاد في فهمنا لهذه الاكتشافات الرائعة.

26

Supporting Growth in the Arts

دعم ازدهار الفنون

Twenty miles southwest of Amman, the city of Madaba is internationally renowned for its 1,500-year history of mosaic art. In 2007, USAID supported the Madaba Institute for Mosaic Art and Restoration, which is dedicated to the study and restoration of ancient mosaics and preservation of Jordan's rich mosaic heritage. Through this institute, the Madaba Mosaic School established a formal diploma program in the production and restoration of mosaic art. Hundreds of students have since studied mosaic production, and the school has helped train a new generation of Jordanian artisans and conservators, ensuring that the intricate art of mosaic making continues to thrive.

على بُعد عشرين ميلًا جنوب غرب عمان، تقع مدينة مادبا التي تشتهر بفن الفسيفساء منذ 1500 عام مضى. وفي عام 2007، دعمت الوكالة الأميركية للتنمية الدولية معهد مادبا لفن الفسيفساء والترميم، الذي يكرس نفسه لدراسة وترميم الفسيفساء القديمة والحفاظ على التراث الغني للفسيفساء في الأردن. ومن خلال هذا المعهد، أسست مدرسةُ الفسيفساء في مادبا برنامجَ دبلوم في إنتاج فن الفسيفساء وترميمها. ومنذ ذلك الحين، درس مئات الطلاب فن الفسيفساء، وساعدت المدرسة في تدريب جيل جديد من الحرفيين الأردنيين وفنيي الحفاظ على الفسيفساء، ما يضمن استمرار ازدهار فن صناعة الفسيفساء الغني بالتفاصيل.

27

Conserving Desert Castles

حفظ القصور الصحراوية

Amid the stark and expansive desert landscape of eastern Jordan sits Qusayr Amra, Jordan's best-known desert castle. Built in the 740s CE, it is one of the country's designated UNESCO World Heritage sites. From 2011 to 2015, a U.S. Department of State's Ambassador's Fund for Cultural Preservation project to protect and conserve Qusayr Amra funded structural conservation, new window installation, and ceiling coverings to prevent degradation from the environment. The project also added interpretation panels, conserved Arabic inscriptions, and re-treated prior conservation methods, revealing rich colors and offering a unique glimpse into the cultural and artistic achievements of the Umayyad period. Exterior restoration, mural conservation, and archaeological surveys were preludes to laser scanning of the site, to record it in perpetuity.

وسط المشهد الصحراوي القاحل الفسيح في شرق الأردن، يقوم قُصير عمرة، وهو أشهر القصور الصحراوية في الأردن، بني في سبعينات القرن الثامن الميلادي، وهو أحد المواقع المدرجة على قائمة اليونسكو للتراث العالمي. ومن عام 2011 إلى 2015، مول مشروع صندوق السفراء الأميركي للحفاظ على التراث الثقافي أعمال حماية قُصير عمرة وترميمه، وخُصص التمويل لأعمال الحفاظ الهيكلي، وتركيب نوافذ جديدة، وتغطية الأسطح لحمايتها من تأثيرات البيئة. كما أضاف المشروع لوحات تفسيرية، ورمم النقوش العربية، وأعيدت معالجة أساليب الترميم السابقة، ما كشف عن الألوان الغنية للوحات الجدارية، وأتاح إطلالة فريدة على الإنجازات الثقافية والفنية في الفترة الأموية. وأجريت أعمال ترميم خارجية، وأعمال حفاظ على الجداريات، ومسوح أثرية تمهيدًا لعملية المسح بالليزر للموقع، لتوثيقه للأجيال القادمة.

Understanding Life in the Desert

فهم الحياة في الصحراء

Thriving in a desert requires special skills, and these have been honed in the far reaches of Jordan for millennia. Past generations have left traces in the sands as a reminder to us today of what has been and can be. In 2022, USAID supported production of a book titled *The Archaeological and Tourism Reality in the Eastern Desert*. The work analyzes the archaeological sites in the Eastern Badia region of Jordan, documenting and reassessing their historical and cultural significance while exploring the potential for tourism development. Written in Arabic, the book makes this information more widely accessible to local audiences and highlights the relationship between archaeology and tourism, emphasizing how promotion of these sites can contribute to cultural heritage preservation and to local economies. The monumental Islamic-era Qasr Harrana, a desert castle with two levels comprised of 60 rooms and a rainwater collection pool at its center, was built in the 7th century CE and likely served as a meeting space for local tribes.

يتطلب العيش في الصحراء مهارات خاصة صقلها الإنسان في الأردن على مدار آلاف السنين. وخلَّفت لنا الأجيال الماضية في الرمال آثارًا لتكون ذكرى، لما كان، وما يمكن أن يكون. وفي عام 2022، دعمت الوكالة الأميركية للتنمية الدولية إنتاج كتاب بعنوان "الواقع الأثري والسياحي في البادية الشرقية"، درس المواقع الأثرية في البادية الشرقية بالأردن، موثِّقًا لها، ومعيدًا تقييم أهميتها التاريخية والثقافية، ومستكشفًا لإمكانيات تطوير السياحة فيها. وصدر الكتاب باللغة العربية، ما يسهل الوصول إلى هذه المعلومات على المستوى المحلي، ويشجع على النمو الاقتصادي. ويسلط الكتاب الضوء على العلاقة بين علم الآثار والسياحة، مؤكدًا أن الترويج لهذه المواقع يسهم في الحفاظ على التراث الثقافي وفي دعم الاقتصاد المحلي. ومن المعالم البارزة في الكتاب قصر الخَرَّانة الذي يعود إلى العصر الإسلامي، والمكون من طابقين، فيهما 60 غرفة، وفي وسطه بركة لجمع مياه الأمطار. وقد بني القصر في القرن السابع الميلادي، وربما كان مكانًا تجتمع فيه القبائل المحلية.

30

Conserving an Umayyad Palace

(left, upper)
Qasr Al-Mushatta stands as a magnificent relic of early Islamic architecture. Intended as a winter retreat for Umayyad caliphs, this palace, built in the 700s CE and never fully completed, was adorned with a grandiose facade, intricate stone carvings, and geometric patterns. In 2019 and 2023, the U.S. Department of State's Ambassador's Fund for Cultural Preservation (AFCP) funded the conservation of the palace ruins and development of a site management plan to allow future generations to visit this desert castle. Currently on UNESCO's tentative list for inclusion as a World Heritage Site, Qasr Al-Mushatta is closer to achieving this prestigious recognition because of the AFCP-funded work.

Excavating Crusader Castles

(left, lower)
The imposing stone citadel of Karak Castle, a medieval crusader fortress located halfway between Amman and Aqaba, has stood witness to nearly a millennium of history. Castle construction began in 1140 by Pagan the Butler, lord of Oultrejordain (what is today much of southern Jordan) and King Fulk of Jerusalem. From this location rulers could control the trade route between Mecca and Damascus. During the Third Crusade, Karak Castle was besieged by the sultan Saladin, founder of the Ayyubid dynasty. In the 1960s, USAID supported excavations and reconstruction of sections of the castle walls, ensuring its preservation for centuries to come.

الحفاظ على قصر أموي

(أقصى اليسار)
يقف قصر المشتى شاهدًا رائعًا على عمارة العصر الإسلامي المبكر، وكان من المقرر أن يكون هذا القصر الذي بني في السبعينات من القرن السابع الميلادي ولم يكتمل بناؤه، منتجعًا شتويًا للخلفاء الأمويين. زُيِّن القصر بواجهة فخمة، وبنقوش حجرية كثيرة التفاصيل، وبأنماط هندسية. وفي عامي 2019 و2023، موَّل صندوق السفراء للحفاظ على التراث الثقافي أعمال الحفاظ على أنقاض القصر وتطوير خطة لإدارة الموقع، ما سيتيح للأجيال القادمة زيارة هذا القصر الصحراوي. وحاليًا، قصر المشتى مدرج في القائمة المؤقتة لليونسكو تمهيدًا لإدراجه كموقع تراث عالمي، وأصبح أقرب إلى تحقيق هذا الإنجاز المرموق بفضل أعمال الترميم الممولة من الصندوق.

التنقيبات الأثرية في قلعة الكرك

(أدنى اليسار)
تُعد قلعة الكرك الحجرية المهيبة شاهدة على ما يقارب ألف عام من التاريخ، وهي حصن صليبي يقع بين عمان والعقبة. بدأ بناؤها في عام 1140 ميلادي على يد باغان النادل، لورد أولترجوردين (التي تشمل معظم جنوب الأردن اليوم)، والملك فولك ملك القدس، وكانت تتحكم في الطريق التجاري الواصل بين مكة ودمشق. وخلال الحملة الصليبية الثالثة، حاصرها السلطان صلاح الدين، مؤسس الدولة الأيوبية. وفي الستينات من القرن الماضي، دعمت الوكالة الأميركية للتنمية الدولية التنقيبات الأثرية في القلعة وإعادة بناء أجزاء من أسوارها، ما ضمن الحفاظ عليها لقرون قادمة.

Preserving Petra's Temple of the Winged Lions

(right, upper)

Deep in the heart of the city of Petra, the commanding remains of the enigmatic Temple of the Winged Lions peer down on the ancient economic center from a ridge above. From 2011 to 2024, two U.S. Department of State's Ambassador's Fund for Cultural Preservation awards, assistance from the U.S. National Endowment for the Humanities, and USAID funding supported the comprehensive study of one of few extant Nabatean temples. The resulting documentation and analysis and comprehensive site management publications have guided community involvement, infrastructure development, conservation, and educational programs to enhance awareness of the importance of cultural heritage preservation among local communities. A two-volume book was published in 2024, recounting the temple's story through its artifacts and architecture.

Safeguarding Byzantine Heritage Sites

(right, lower)

The ancient city of Madaba in central Jordan has long been renowned for its arts, particularly mosaics. Development of the area in the 1980s and 1990s resulted in the discovery of many important monuments, including the Burnt Palace, thought to be a Byzantine-era residence from the 6th or 7th century CE. Ravaged by fires caused by an ancient earthquake, the palace is notable for its well-preserved mosaics, which feature arrays of engaging scenes and motifs and showcase the artistic skills and life of that era. In 1990, USAID funded a protective cover, which helps preserve these mosaics from weather-related deterioration and provides a controlled environment for visitors, allowing them to appreciate the historical significance of the site and the beauty of its details.

الحفاظ على معبد الأسود المجنحة في بترا

(أقصى اليمين)

في قلب مدينة بترا، تطل بقايا معبد الأسود المجنحة الغامض من مرتفعها على مركز المدينة الاقتصادي القديم. ومن 2011 إلى 2024، دعم صندوق السفراء للحفاظ على التراث الثقافي، والوكالة الأميركية للتنمية الدولية، والصندوق الوطني للعلوم الإنسانية إعداد خطط للإدارة الشاملة للموارد الثقافية، والدراسة، والنشر لهذا المعلم المهم، والذي يُعد واحدًا من المعابد النبطية القليلة المعروفة. وشملت الأعمال مشاركة مجتمعية مدروسة، وتطوير البنية التحتية، والحفاظ على المعلم، وتنفيذ برامج تعليمية لزيادة الوعي لدى المجتمع المحلي بأهمية الحفاظ على التراث الثقافي، ما ساهم في تعزيز تجربة الزوار، وحماية هذا الموقع الأثري المدهش في الوقت نفسه. ونُشر كتاب من جزئين في عام 2024 يروي قصة عمارة المعبد وما اكتُشف فيه من لقى أثرية.

حماية المعالم الأثرية القديمة

(أدنى اليمين)

تشتهر مدينة مادبا القديمة الواقعة وسط الأردن منذ زمن بعيد بفنونها، وخاصة بوصفها مركزًا للفنون الفسيفسائية. وشهدت المنطقة في الثمانينات والتسعينات من القرن الماضي اكتشاف العديد من الآثار المهمة، بما في ذلك البناء المسمى "القصر المحترق"، الذي يُعتقد أنه كان مسكنًا من العصر البيزنطي (القرن السادس أو السابع الميلادي). وتعرض القصر للدمار بسبب حرائق ناجمة عن زلزال قديم، ويتميز بالفسيفساء المحفوظة بشكل جيد، التي تعرض مشاهد وأنماطًا زخرفية مثيرة، ما يعكس المهارات الفنية والحياة في تلك الحقبة. وفي عام 1990، قدمت الوكالة الأميركية للتنمية الدولية تمويلًا لإنشاء سقف واقٍ، ساعد في الحفاظ على هذه الأرضيات الفسيفسائية من التدهور الناتج عن الظروف الجوية، ووفّر بيئة مضبوطة للزوار، ما يسمح لهم بتقدير الأهمية التاريخية للموقع وجمال تفاصيله.

33

Preserving the "Founder's Tomb" in Ancient Capitolias

الحفاظ على "قبر المؤسس" في كابيتولياس القديمة

The Roman city of Capitolias, now modern-day Bayt Ras, stood at the crossroads of several ancient territories. Unique in its relatively recent and well-documented founding (around 97 CE), the city provides a glimpse of a dynamic time and place that witnessed majors shifts of empires and peoples alike. From 2017 to 2020, USAID supported an international consortium's efforts to enhance the site's physical security and a series of architectural, archaeological, and epigraphic surveys of its uniquely frescoed "founder's tomb," dating to the 1st century CE. Lavish paintings on the walls tell the story of the establishment of Capitolias. The topographic maps, laser scans, and models of the tomb resulting from the project have allowed students, experts, and archaeology enthusiasts to learn more about this ancient city of the Decapolis, a famous confederation of ten cities in this region of the Roman Empire's eastern frontier. The site was featured in a 2024 National Geographic television documentary titled "Rome's Desert Cities."

تقع مدينة كابيتولياس الرومانية، المعروفة اليوم ببيت راس، عند تقاطع عدة مناطق قديمة، وهي فريدة من نوعها، لأنها بُنيت في وقت متأخر نسبيًا (حوالي عام 97 ميلادي)، ولأنها موثقة توثيقًا جيدًا، ما يوفر للزوار لمحة عن مكان شهد تحولات كبيرة في الإمبراطوريات والشعوب على حد سواء. ومن عام 2017 إلى 2020، قدمت الوكالة الأميركية للتنمية الدولية تمويلًا لدعم جهود ائتلاف دولي عمل على تعزيز الاستقرار الفيزيائي، وإجراء سلسلة من المسوحات المعمارية والأثرية، ودراسة للنقوش في "مدفن المؤسس" الفريد المزخرف بالفسيفساء، والذي يعود إلى القرن الأول الميلادي. وتروي اللوحات الفاخرة على جدران القبر قصة تأسيس كابيتولياس. وقد أتاحت الخرائط الطبوغرافية، والمسح بالليزر، والنماذج الناتجة عن المشروع للطلاب، والخبراء، والهواة التعرف بشكل أعمق على هذه المدينة القديمة من مدن اتحاد الديكابوليس، وهو اتحاد شهير من عشر مدن قام على الحدود الشرقية للإمبراطورية الرومانية. وقد عُرض الموقع في فيلم وثائقي بثته قناة ناشيونال جيوغرافيك في عام 2024 بعنوان "مدن روما الصحراوية".

35

Recording Local Traditions for Future Generations

توثيق التقاليد المحلية للأجيال القادمة

Understanding the history of a place includes understanding the accounts of its people. In 1991, the U.S. National Endowment for the Humanities funded "A Cultural History of the Bedouin of Southern Jordan," a study that explored the rich traditions, social structures, and cultural practices of the Bedouin communities, particularly in areas such as Petra and Wadi Rum. The Bedouin of Jordan have played critical roles in the region's changes and developments throughout the historic era, and documenting their customs and heritage is critical to long-term preservation of Bedouin culture and a holistic understanding of the region.

فهم تاريخ المكان يشمل فهم تاريخ شعوبه؛ ففي عام 1991، مول الصندوق الوطني للعلوم الإنسانية دراسة بعنوان "التاريخ الثقافي للبدو في جنوب الأردن"، وهي دراسة استكشفت التقاليد الغنية، والتنظيمات المجتمعية، والممارسات الثقافية للمجتمعات البدوية، لا سيما في مناطق، مثل بترا ووادي رم. ولعب البدو في الأردن دورًا حاسمًا في التغييرات والتطورات في المنطقة عبر العصور التاريخية، لكنهم كانوا أقل ظهورًا في السجل الثقافي مقارنةً بثقافات أخرى، علمًا أن توثيق أنماط حياتهم أمر بالغ الأهمية، ليس للحفاظ عليها على المدى الطويل وحسب، وإنما لفهم شامل ومتكامل للمنطقة عمومًا.

Preserving Intangible Heritage

توثيق التراث اللامادي

Among the ruins, sites, artifacts, and texts that illuminate past civilizations, much can be lost to time, especially the intangible heritage—the sounds, smells, dialects, cuisine, and customs that can define daily cultural experiences. In 2021, USAID helped preserve Jordanian intangible cultural heritage by reviving the rich tradition of folk songs from the Governorate of Jerash and capturing the melodies and oral traditions passed down through generations. The project not only safeguarded an important aspect of Jordan's living heritage but also fostered an intergenerational appreciation for the art of storytelling through song.

الخرائب، والمواقع الأثرية، واللقى القديمة، والكتابات كلها جزء من التراث المادي الذي يمثل ماضينا. ولكنْ، وإن حفظنا هذه الآثار كلها، فقد تضيع بمرور الزمن أشياء أخرى عديدة، هي التراث اللامادي، كالأصوات، والروائح، واللهجات، والأطباق التي نختبرها يوميًا. وفي عام 2021، ساهمت الوكالة الأميركية للتنمية الدولية في الحفاظ على التراث الثقافي اللامادي الأردني من خلال إحياء تقليد الأغاني الشعبية في محافظة جرش، وتوثيق الألحان والتقاليد الشفهية التي تتناقلها الأجيال. ولم يقتصر المشروع على الحفاظ على جانب مهم من تراث الأردن الحي فحسب، بل ساهم أيضًا في تعزيز تقدير الأجيال المختلفة لفن السرد القصصي من خلال الأغاني.

37

38

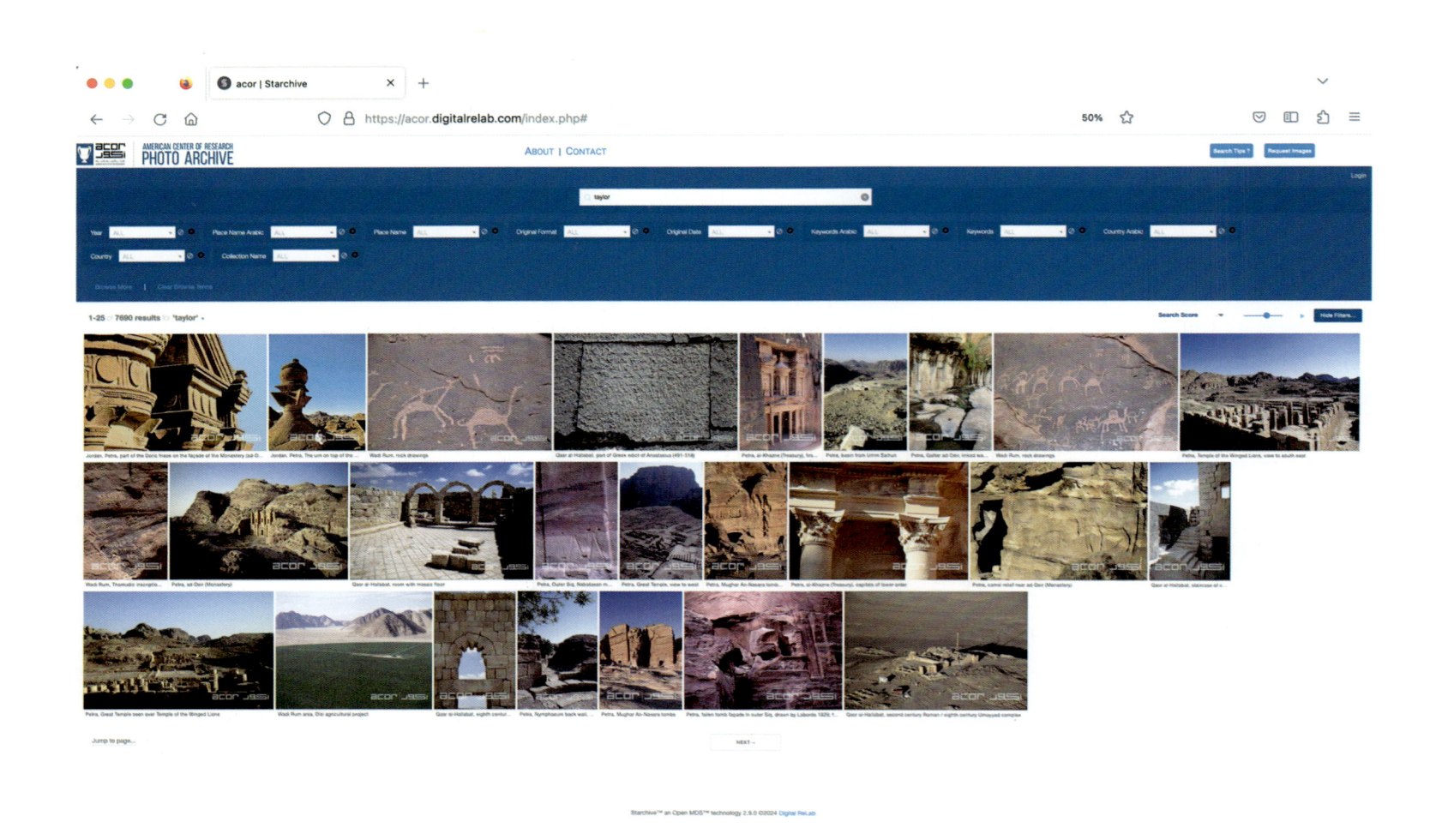

Supporting Foundational Research and Discoveries

(left, upper)
From 1983 to 2013, collaborative effort between U.S. Information Agency, the U.S. National Science Foundation, the Binational Fulbright Commission, and other partners supported six groundbreaking archaeological projects in the Wadi Hasa area of the southern Dead Sea. These excavations investigated various aspects of Late Pleistocene-era and Early Holocene-era hunter-gatherer structures that date back 11,500 years. The projects engaged community members, developed local research capacity, provided material aid to farming operations, and instructed students at universities in Jordan about the discoveries at the site.

Providing Digital Resources in a Technological Age

(left, lower)
Technical advances throughout the past century have resulted in an exponential increase of digital recordkeeping. However, organizing and accessing these records remains a challenge. Since 2014, the U.S. Department of Education has funded the creation and expansion of a groundbreaking digital archive, now the single largest repository for historic media from Jordan. With nearly 100,000 still images, videos, audio recordings, and archival documents, this comprehensive collection offers a rich, accessible resource for educators, scholars, and the public. It provides a unique opportunity to explore and understand the past and present of Jordan through a wealth of visual and historical material. This invaluable archive is available for free at digitalarchive.acorjordan.org.

دعم البحث والاكتشافات المؤسسية

(أقصى اليسار)
من عام 1983 إلى عام 2013، دعمت الجهود المشتركة لوكالة المعلومات الأميركية، والمؤسسة الوطنية للعلوم، ولجنة فولبرايت، وشركاء آخرون ستة مشاريع أثرية رائدة في منطقة وادي الحسا جنوب البحر الميت. ودرست هذه التنقيبات المنشآت التي أقامها الصيادون وجامعو الثمار في أواخر عصر البلايستوسين وأوائل عصر الهولوسين من جوانبها المختلفة، والتي يعود تاريخها إلى 11,500 عام. وأشركت المشاريع أبناء المجتمع المحلي في أعمالها، ما ساهم في تطوير القدرات البحثية المحلية، وقدم المساعدة العينية الزراعة، ودرَّست الطلاب في الجامعات الأردنية عن الاكتشافات التي أُجريت في الموقع.

توفير الموارد الرقمية في العصر الرقمي

(أدنى اليسار)
شهد القرن الماضي تقدمًا تكنولوجيًا هائلًا، أدى إلى تضاعف السجلات التاريخية والمعاصرة بشكل كبير، حتى صار تنظيم هذه السجلات والوصول إليها تحديًا للمشتغلين بها. ومنذ عام 2014، موَّلت وزارة التعليم الأميركية إنشاء وتوسيع أرشيف رقمي رائد، يُعد الآن أكبر مستودع للوسائط التاريخية من الأردن. ويضم هذا الأرشيف الشامل ما يقرب من 100,000 صورة، ومقطع فيديو، وتسجيل صوتي، ووثائق أرشيفية، ما يوفر موردًا غنيًا متاحًا للمعلمين، والباحثين، والجمهور على حد سواء. ويتيح هذا الأرشيف فرصة فريدة لاستكشاف ماضي الأردن وحاضره وفهمهما، من خلال ثروة من المواد البصرية والتاريخية. هذا ويُذكر أن هذا الأرشيف القيِّم متاح مجانًا عبر الرابط الآتي: digitalarchive.acorjordan.org

Creating Accessible Tourism

سياحة متاحة للجميع

The Edomites were an ancient Semitic people who played a pivotal role in regional history during the 1st millennium BCE. Located in the rugged hills of southern Jordan, Busayra was once the capital of their kingdom, a bustling stronghold that controlled key routes through the desert that connected the Arabian Peninsula with the Mediterranean world. USAID support from 2015 to 2019 provided for a deeper understanding of the Edomites by preserving the remnants of their once-mighty kingdom and cooperating with Jordanian partners on interventions such as development of a timeline mural highlighting the significant role the Edomites played in shaping the cultural and political landscape of the ancient Near East, an interpretive trail, and signs that make the site more accessible for tourists to Jordan.

من بين الحضارات القديمة في الأردن كان الإدوميون شعبًا ساميًا قديمًا لعب دورًا محوريًا في تاريخ المنطقة خلال الألفية الأولى قبل الميلاد. وتقع بلدة بصيرا في التلال الوعرة بجنوب الأردن، وكانت عاصمة لمملكة الإدوميين، وحصنًا يشرف على الطرق الرئيسة المارة عبر الصحراء، والتي وصلت جزيرة العرب بالعالم المتوسطي. ومن عام 2015 إلى عام 2019، دعمت الوكالة الأميركية للتنمية الدولية العديد من الجهود الرامية إلى تحقيق فهم أعمق للإدوميين من خلال الحفاظ على بقايا مملكتهم العظيمة، بالإضافة إلى تنفيذ مبادرات، مثل تطوير لوحة جدارية عليها جدول زمني، يبين الدور الكبير الذي لعبه الإدوميون في تشكيل المشهد الثقافي والسياسي للشرق الأدنى القديم. كما دعمت الوكالة إنشاء مسار تفسيري ولوحات إرشادية يسّرت للسائحين إلى الأردن زيارة الموقع.

40

Supporting Small Businesses

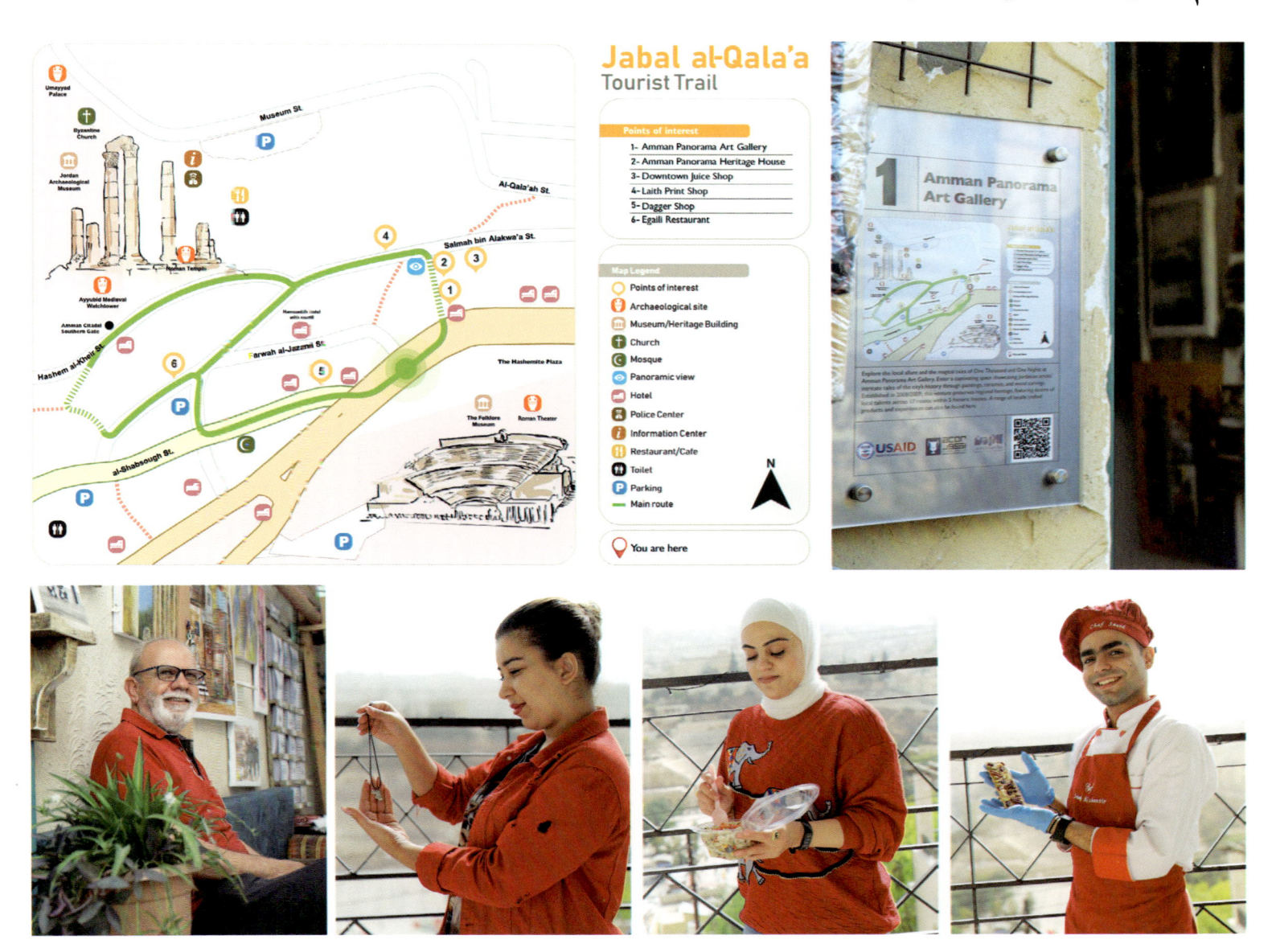

From 2022 to 2024, USAID and the Government of Jordan cooperated to help businesses recover from the challenges of the post-COVID era. One noteworthy initiative was the creation of a new tourism trail at the Amman Citadel, which linked the Citadel and the Roman Theater for the first time in nearly a thousand years. This has allowed visitors to Jordan a seamless journey through history and culture and has allowed local craftsmanship to flourish along this vibrant trail. Jewelers, chocolatiers, artisans, and vendors offer visitors their handmade treasures, from delicate jewelry to mouthwatering sweets and savory delights. This revitalization has not only kept cherished businesses alive but also sparked the emergence of new ones, infusing the historic heart of Amman with a renewed sense of energy and pride.

دعم الشركات الصغيرة وتأسيسها

من عام 2022 إلى عام 2024، دعمت الوكالة الأمريكية للتنمية الدولية قطاع السياحة في الأردن دعمًا أساسيًا بقصد إعادة تنشيطه، ما ساعد الشركات على التعافي من التحديات التي خلقتها جائحة كوفيد-19. ومن أبرز الجهود التي بُذلت في هذا الصدد كان إنشاء مسار سياحي جديد بجبل القلعة في عمان، طُور بالتعاون الوثيق مع الحكومة الأردنية. ولأول مرة منذ ما يقرب من ألف عام، رُبط جبل القلعة بالمدرج الروماني، ما وفر للزوار تجربة سلسة تجمع بين التاريخ والثقافة. وعلى طول هذا المسار النابض بالحياة، تزدهر مشاهد الحرف المحلية، حيث يعرض صائغو المجوهرات، وصانعو الشوكولاتة، والحرفيون، والبائعون كنوزهم اليدوية، من المجوهرات الدقيقة، إلى الحلويات الشهية، والمأكولات المالحة. ولم يسهم هذا التجديد في الحفاظ على الأعمال التجارية القيِّمة فحسب، بل حفز أيضًا ظهور أعمال جديدة، ما بثّ في قلب عمان التاريخي طاقة جديدة وشعورًا متجددًا بالفخر.

Highlighting the Medieval Sugar Factory in Ghor as-Safi

تسليط الضوء على مصنع السكر في غور الصافي من العصور الإسلامية الوسيطة

Nestled in the southeastern corner of the Dead Sea was a sweet enterprise whose exports spanned the region for centuries: a sugar factory. A community-first approach by USAID between 2015 and 2022 focused on the sustainable preservation, management, and promotion of the Masna al-Sukkar (sugar factory) from the medieval Islamic period in the Ghor as-Safi region of Jordan. The project helped the local Jordanian community harness the potential of this cultural heritage resource, creating opportunities for education, employment, and economic growth.

في الزاوية الجنوبية الشرقية من البحر الميت، كانت توجد مؤسسة صناعية حلوة الصيت امتدت صادراتها عبر المنطقة لقرون، ألا وهي مصنع للسكر. ومن عام 2015 إلى عام 2022، قدمت الوكالة الأميركية للتنمية الدولية تمويلًا يدعم نهجًا يركز على المجتمع المحلي في الحفاظ المستدام وإدارة وترويج مصنع السكر الراجع إلى الفترة الإسلامية الوسيطة في منطقة غور الصافي في الأردن. وساعد المشروع المجتمع المحلي على استغلال الإمكانات الكامنة لهذا المورد التراثي الثقافي، فأتاح فرصًا للتعليم، والتوظيف، والنمو الاقتصادي المستقل.

Uncovering History at Tall al-'Umayri

الكشف عن تاريخ تل العُميري

Research support funded under the U.S. Congress' Near and Middle East Research and Training Act resulted in new excavations at Tall al-'Umayri, located on one of the rolling ridges along the Queen Aila Airport Highway. Among the remains discovered at the site in 1999 were a megalithic tomb with the skeletal remains of nearly 30 people, a defensive system, imported goods, a cultic complex, evidence that the ancient town suffered a fiery destruction, and architecture from 1100 BCE into Roman times. All of these findings help impart the complex history of regional societal changes in antiquity.

في عام 1999، دعم الصندوق الوطني الأميركي للبحث والتدريب الأثري الحفريات في تل العُميري، الواقع على تلة متموجة على طريق مطار الملكة علياء. ويحتوي الموقع على قبر حجري كبير، دولمن، يضم رفات حوالي 30 شخصًا، وعلى نظام دفاعي، وبضائع مستوردة، ومجمع ديني، وأدلة على أن حريقًا دمر المدينة القديمة، بالإضافة إلى عمارة تعود إلى الفترة بين عام 1100 قبل الميلاد والعصر الروماني. وتساهم هذه الاكتشافات في رواية التاريخ الكثير التفاصيل للتغيرات المجتمعية التي حدثت في المنطقة خلال العصور القديمة.

Illuminating the "Dark Ages"

إلقاء الضوء على العصور المظلمة

On a ridge overlooking the heart of ancient Petra, excavations in 1992 funded by USAID unearthed what has become known as "the Petra Church," dating to the 5th and 6th century CE. The Petra Authority and Jordan's Department of Antiquities worked in close partnership with the American Center of Research to excavate, conserve, and present to the public this grandly decorated Byzantine-era church. Dozens of elaborate floor mosaics, illustrating the natural world, personifications of the seasons, and more, add to an image of a vibrant world. Discovery in the church of 140 carbonized papyri has fundamentally changed knowledge about the era, depicting a complex and legalistic society during a time about which virtually no other written records exist. The U.S. National Endowment for the Humanities provided the foundations for an endowment that today still supports maintenance of the site and preservation of its scrolls.

على تلة تطل على قلب مدينة بترا القديمة، كشفت التنقيبات التي أُجريت عام 1992 بتمويل من الوكالة الأميركية للتنمية الدولية عما يُعرف الآن بـ "كنيسة بترا" التي تعود إلى القرنين الخامس والسادس الميلاديين. وعملت سلطة بترا ودائرة الآثار العامة بشراكة وثيقة مع المركز الأميركي للأبحاث على التنقيب عن هذه الكنيسة المزخرفة بعظمة من العصر البيزنطي، وترميمها، وتقديمها للجمهور. وتزين الكنيسةَ عشراتُ الأرضيات الفسيفسائية الرائعة التي تصور العالم الطبيعي، وتجسد الفصول، وتتناول غيرها من الموضوعات، ما يعكس صورة عالم نابض بالحياة. واكتُشفت هناك أيضًا 140 بردية متفحمة داخل الكنيسة أدت إلى تغيير جذري في معرفتنا بتلك الحقبة، إذ تسلط الضوء على مجتمع معقد ومنظم قانونيًا في زمن يفتقر إلى أية سجلات مكتوبة أخرى تقريبًا من المنطقة. وقد وفّر تمويل من الصندوق الوطني للعلوم الإنسانية الأساس لوقفية تضمن اليوم صيانة الموقع والحفاظ على الوثائق المكتشفة.

Enhancing Understanding of the Ancient Kingdoms of Jordan

Built on a rugged plateau in the heart of Jordan, Balu'a is an ancient city dating back to the Iron Age. An important site in the kingdom of Moab (9th to 7th centuries BCE), Balu'a was inhabited intermittently by virtually every succeeding culture in Jordan. Starting in 2019, the U.S. National Science Foundation has provided funding to analyze botanical remains from the site to better understand the agricultural heritage of the Iron Age and, through comparison with other regional sites, Jordan more broadly.

Excavating Pella, Hub of the Ancient World

(following pages)
Established in the richly fertile northern Jordan Valley, the ancient city of Pella is one of Jordan's most significant archaeological sites, boasting a history of human presence stretching back to the 6th millennium BCE. Its famous rows of columns mark the construction of a Byzantine church. Below the church, built into the hillside, lies a small Roman theater where an audience of up to 400 people would gather for musical performances. The U.S. National Endowment for the Humanities has provided multiple grants in support of archaeological excavations at Pella involving many Jordanian and international partners since 1979.

تعزيز فهمنا للممالك القديمة في الأردن

تأسس موقع البالوع على هضبة وعرة في قلب الأردن، وهو مدينة قديمة تعود إلى العصر الحديدي، وتُعد موقعًا مهمًا في مملكة مؤاب (من القرن التاسع إلى القرن السابع قبل الميلاد)، وسكنتها بشكل متقطع كل الحضارات التي جاءت بعد ذلك في الأردن. وبدءًا من عام 2019، قدمت المؤسسة الوطنية للعلوم تمويلًا لتحليل البقايا النباتية من الموقع بهدف فهم التراث الزراعي للعصر الحديدي في البالوع بشكل أفضل من خلال المقارنة مع مواقع أخرى، بقصد فهم تاريخ الزراعة في الأردن بشكل أوسع.

التنقيبات الأثرية في بيلا (محطة قوافل العالم القديم)

(يتبع في الصفحات التالية)
تأسست مدينة بيلا القديمة في وادي الأردن الشمالي الخصب، وهي واحدة من أهم المواقع الأثرية في الأردن، إذ يرجع تاريخ وجود الإنسان فيها إلى الألفية السادسة قبل الميلاد. وتشير صفوف الأعمدة الشهيرة في الموقع إلى وجود كنيسة بيزنطية، وأسفل الكنيسة المبنية في التل، يقع مسرح روماني صغير، حيث كان يتجمع جمهور يصل عدده إلى 400 شخص للاستماع بالعروض الموسيقية. وقدمت المؤسسة الوطنية للإنسانيات منذ عام 1979 العديد من المنح لدعم التنقيبات الأثرية في بيلا بالتعاون مع العديد من الشركاء الدوليين.

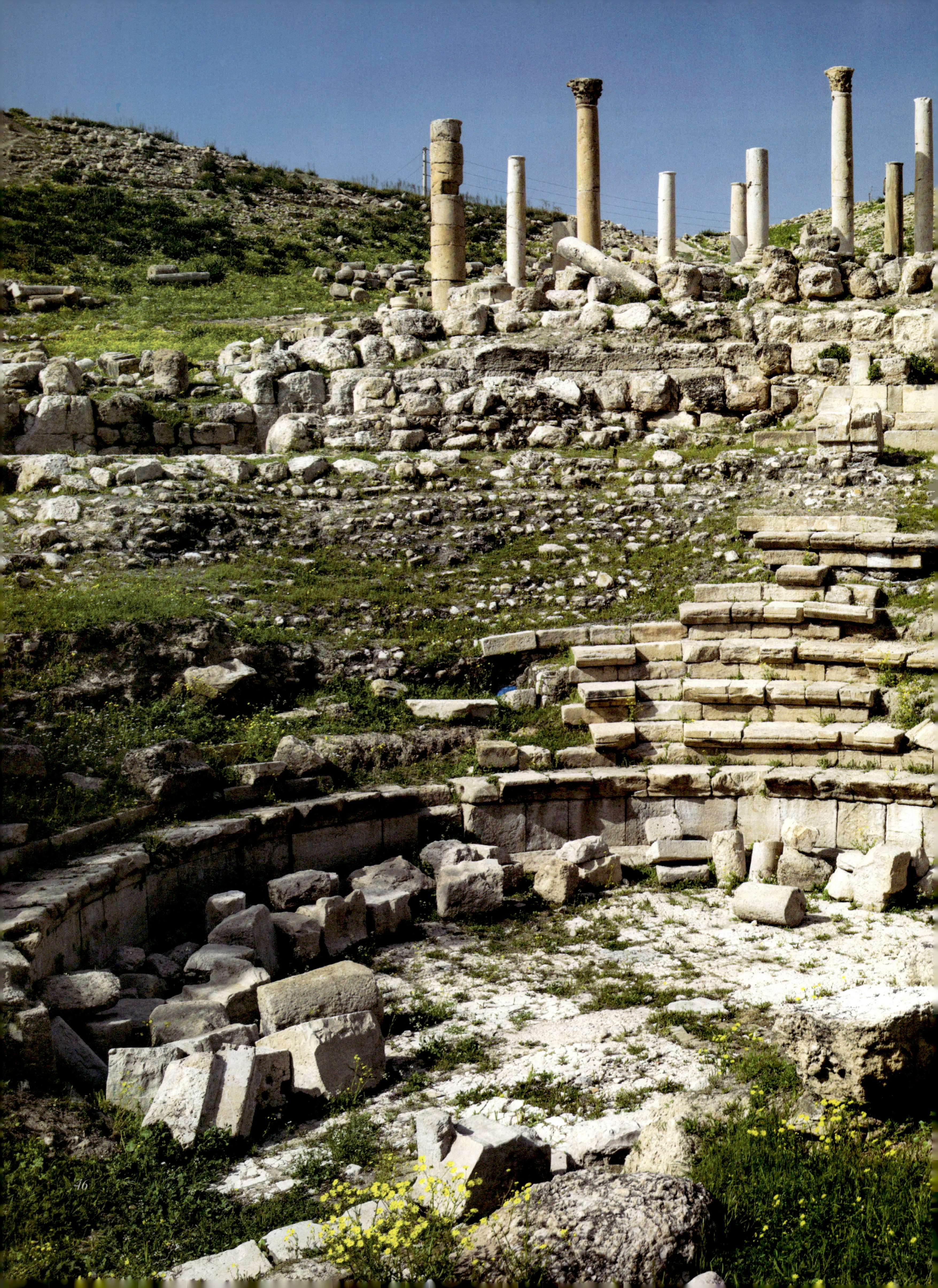

47

Fostering Intellectual Exchange

دعم التبادل الفكري

People-to-people engagement and knowledge sharing are foundational to the U.S.-Jordan relationship. In 2007, 2016, and 2019, the U.S. Embassy in Amman and USAID supported the International Conference on the History and Archaeology of Jordan (ICHAJ), prestigious triennial academic gatherings held under the auspices of HRH Prince El Hassan bin Talal that convene students, scholars, researchers, and experts to discuss and share insights on Jordan's rich historical and archaeological heritage. George Washington University hosted the 2007 conference, which received royal patronage from HRH Princess Sumaya bint El Hassan.

التفاعل بين الأشخاص وتشارك المعرفة هو أساس العلاقة الأردنية الأميركية. وفي أعوام 2007 و2016 و2019، دعمَت السفارة الأميركية بعمّان والوكالة الأميركية للتنمية الدولية المؤتمر الدولي لتاريخ الأردن وآثاره (ICHAJ)، وهو تجمع أكاديمي مرموق يُعقد مرة كل ثلاث سنوات برعاية صاحب السمو الملكي الأمير الحسن بن طلال، يلتقي فيه الطلاب، والعلماء، والباحثون، والخبراء لمناقشة رؤاهم وتشاركها حول التراث التاريخي والأثري الغني للأردن. واستضافت جامعة جورج واشنطن المؤتمر عام 2007 الذي حظي برعاية ملكية من صاحبة السمو الملكي الأميرة سمية بنت الحسن.

48

Elevating Standards of Tourism

رفع معايير السياحة

Showcasing Jordan's cultural richness to domestic and international visitors requires tourism professionals with the skills and knowledge to deliver world-class services. To further strengthen Jordan's tourism economy, a project supported by USAID from 2008 to 2012 delivered training modules tailored to the unique demands of the industry, empowering Jordan's tourism workforce to provide visitors with a more engaging experience. This investment in one of Jordan's biggest resources—its human capital—has helped position Jordan as a competitive and attractive destination on the global stage.

يتطلب إبراز غنى الأردن الثقافي للزوار المحليين والدوليين وجود محترفين في مجال السياحة، يمتلكون المهارات والمعرفة اللازمة لتقديم خدمات عالمية المستوى. ولتعزيز اقتصاد السياحة في الأردن، نفذَ مشروع مدعوم من الوكالة الأميركية للتنمية الدولية بين عامي 2008 و2012 برامج تدريبية مصممة لتلبية المتطلبات الفريدة للقطاع، ما مكّن القوى العاملة بمجال السياحة في الأردن من تقديم تجربة أكثر إثراءً للزوار. وساهم هذا الاستثمار في واحدة من أكبر موارد الأردن - رأس المال البشري - في تعزيز مكانة الأردن كوجهة تنافسية وجذابة على الساحة العالمية.

49

Interpreting History through Ceramics

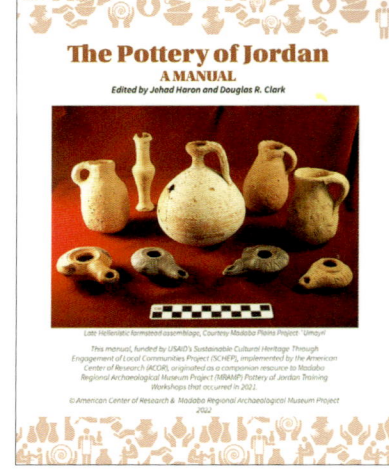

تفسير تاريخ المنطقة من الفخار

Examining and understanding a region's ceramics, which are often the most common finds from the past, allows historians and archaeologists to trace chronologies, technologies, and trade routes. Archaeologists study the materials, decorations, and shapes of potsherds and whole objects to reveal information about where, when, why, and by whom they were made. From 2018 to 2021, USAID supported the publication of the first manual of Jordan's pottery. The Arabic and English editions provide museum personnel, archaeologists, students, and other specialists with the first holistic treatment of Jordan's ceramic repertoire in illustrated print and open-access electronic formats. The manual has already become the standard reference resource on Jordanian pottery for ongoing archaeological research and cultural heritage preservation.

تتيح دراسة الفخار وفهمه، والذي يُعَدُّ من أكثر مكتشفات الماضي شيوعًا، للمؤرخين وعلماء الآثار تتبع التسلسل الزمني، وتحديد التقنيات، وطرق التجارة. ويدرس علماء الآثار المواد التي صُنع منها الفخار، وزخارفه، وأشكال قطع الفخار والأواني الكاملة للكشف معلومات عن مكان وزمان صناعتها، وأسبابها، وهوية صانعيها. وبين عامي 2018 و2021، دعمت الوكالة الأميركية للتنمية الدولية نشر أول دليل شامل لفخار الأردن، باللغتين العربية والإنجليزية، يتيح لموظفي المتاحف، وعلماء الآثار، والطلاب، وغيرهم من المختصين أول معالجة شاملة للفخار الأردني، في صورتين مطبوعة وإلكترونية متاحة للجميع. وقد أصبح هذا الدليل المرجع لفخار الأردن في البحث الأثري وحفظ التراث الثقافي الأردني.

Preserving the Palace at Iraq al-Amir

الحفاظ على القصر في عراق الأمير

Rising out of the hills just west of Amman is the site of Iraq al-Amir ("Caves of the Prince"). From the 1970s to the early 2000s, the U.S. National Endowment for the Humanities and the U.S. Department of State provided several grants and other support for excavations here. Named for ten nearby caves with historic evidence of human use, Iraq al-Amir boasts impressive Hellenistic architecture, particularly Qasr al-Abd ("Castle of the Slave"), a large palace from the 2nd century BCE likely built by the Tobiad dynasty. Its pale limestone walls contrast strikingly with the lush, green landscape from which they rise.

يتوسط موقع عراق الأمير (الذي يعني "مغارات الأمير") التلال الواقعة غربي عمان. ومن السبعينات حتى أوائل العقد 2000، قدمت المؤسسة الوطنية للإنسانيات ووزارة الخارجية الأميركية عدة منح وأشكالًا أخرى من الدعم للتنقيبات في هذا الموقع. وسُمي الموقع باسمه هذا نسبة إلى عشر مغارات قريبة منه، استخدمها الإنسان مدة طويلة. ويتميز عراق الأمير بهندسة معمارية هلنستية رائعة، وبأهمية تاريخية استثنائية، وخاصة "قصر العبد"، وهو قصر كبير يعود إلى القرن الثاني قبل الميلاد، يُحتمل أنه بُني على يد سلالة الطوبيين. ويتباين لون جدرانه المصنوعة من الحجر الجيري الفاتح بشكل لافت مع المشاهد الطبيعية الخضراء التي تقوم عليها.

Reassessing History

مراجعة التاريخ

Grants from the U.S. National Endowment for the Humanities and the U.S. Department of State in 1984, 2008, 2016, and 2024 supported excavation at and further study of Khirbet Iskandar, a settlement site tucked in a valley along the ancient King's Highway. Discoveries at the site led to a reconceptualization of the patterns of establishment and abandonment of some early cities. The project engaged local Jordanians and underscored the importance of cultural heritage resources in local development.

منذ عام 1984، دعمت مِنحُ المؤسسة الوطنية للإنسانيات والمركز الأميركي للأبحاث (من خلال منحة مخصصة من مجلس مراكز البحوث الأميركية الخارجية) التنقيبات والدراسات الأثرية في خربة إسكندر، الواقعة في وادٍ على طول الطريق التجاري القديم المعروف بـ"الطريق الملوكي". وتُظهر الاكتشافات في الموقع استمرار الاستقرار من أواخر العصر البرونزي المبكر حتى بداية العصر البرونزي المبكر الرابع، ما يساهم في إعادة تقييم فهمنا لنشأة المدن المبكرة واندثارها. بالإضافة إلى ذلك، يعزز المشروع تنمية موارد التراث الثقافي المحلي، من خلال إشراكه للمجتمع المحلي في أعمال التنقيب والحفاظ.

Conserving a Temple of Artemis

الحفاظ على معبد أرتيمس

Located within one of the best-preserved ancient Roman provincial towns in the world, the 2nd-century CE Temple of Artemis in Jerash was dedicated to the goddess of the hunt, nature, children, and childbirth. From 2018 to 2022, the U.S. Department of State's Ambassador's Fund for Cultural Preservation contributed to the conservation of this impressive testament to Roman architectural prowess and ancient religious devotion, preserving it from further deterioration. Undertaken in cooperation with Jordan's Department of Antiquities, the project reinforced the temple's stone structures and bolstered economic opportunities for the local community by building Jordanians' skills in cultural heritage and increasing tourism to the site.

يقع معبد أرتيمس في جرش، ضمن واحدة من أفضل المدن الرومانية القديمة للمحفوظة في العالم، ويعود تاريخه إلى القرن الثاني الميلادي. كُرِّس المعبد للإلهة أرتميس، إلهة الصيد، والطبيعة، والأطفال، والولادة. ومن 2018 إلى 2022، ساهم صندوق السفراء للحفاظ على التراث الثقافي في صيانة هذا المعلم الرائع الذي يبرز براعة المعمار الروماني والتفاني الديني القديم، ما ساعد في حمايته من المزيد من التدهور. ونُفذ المشروع بالتعاون مع دائرة الآثار العامة، ولم يقتصر العمل على تعزيز الهياكل الحجرية للمعبد فحسب، بل ساعد المشروع أيضًا في تعزيز الفرص الاقتصادية للمجتمع المحلي من خلال تنمية مهارات أفراده في مجال التراث الثقافي، كما ساهم في زيادة السياحة إلى الموقع.

Founding a New Natural Heritage Museum

إنشاء متحف جديد للتراث الطبيعي

Jordan's Al-Hussein Bin Talal University Natural Science Museum is the first museum in southern Jordan to highlight its treasures of biodiversity and natural heritage. The brainchild of the university's faculty of science, the museum—supported by USAID in 2022—offers displays of taxidermy mounts, botanical specimens, photographs, and videos that serve as educational tools for local students and for visitors from around the world. Examining specimens up close can inspire a desire to connect with the natural world, a fundamental element of Jordan's heritage.

يُعَدُّ متحف العلوم الطبيعية في جامعة الحسين بن طلال أول متحف في جنوب الأردن يبرز كنوزه من التنوع البيولوجي والتراث الطبيعي في المنطقة المحيطة. وكان المتحف من بنات أفكار كلية العلوم في الجامعة، وحظي بدعم الوكالة الأمريكية للتنمية الدولية في عام 2022. ويعرض المتحف حيوانات محنطة، ونباتات، وصورًا فوتوغرافية، وفيديوهات تُستخدم كأدوات تعليمية للطلاب المحليين والزوار من مختلف أنحاء العالم. ويمكن أن يُلهم الاطلاع على هذه العينات عن كثب الرغبة لدى الزائرين للاتصال بالعالم الطبيعي، والتعرف على عنصر أساسي من تراث الأردن.

Maintaining a Public Research Library

صيانة مكتبة عامة للأبحاث

Since the 1980s, USAID's American Schools and Hospitals Abroad (ASHA) initiative has played a key role in supporting a variety of endeavors across Jordan. One notable example is its support for the American Center of Research (ACOR), which opened the doors of its current building in 1986 with ASHA funding. ACOR is home to one of Jordan's public libraries, a vital resource that has welcomed tens of thousands of visitors. Boasting more than 45,000 volumes, it stands as one of the largest English-language resources in the Middle East. ACCR's mission remains focused on advancing research, education, and understanding of Jordan's rich history and its dynamic role in the region.

منذ الثمانينات، ساهمت مبادرة لجمعية المدارس والمستشفيات الأميركية في الخارج والتابعة للوكالة الأميركية للتنمية الدولية مساهمة رئيسة في دعم مجموعة متنوعة من المشاريع في الأردن. ومن أبرز الأمثلة على ذلك دعمها للمركز الأميركي للأبحاث، الذي افتتح مبناه الحالي عام 1986 بتمويل من الجمعية. ويُعد المركز موطنًا لإحدى المكتبات العامة في الأردن، وهي مصدر حيوي للمعلومات استقبلت منذ تأسيسها عشرات الآلاف من الزوار. وباشتمالها على أكثر من 45,000 مجلد، فالمكتبة واحدة من أكبر مصادر المعرفة باللغة الإنجليزية في الشرق الأوسط. وتظل مهمة المركز تعزيز فهم التاريخ الغني للأردن ودوره الديناميكي في المنطقة.

Sustaining Cultural Heritage through Engagement of Local Communities

Cultural heritage preservation thrives when it is a shared endeavor, drawing on the knowledge, traditions, and stewardship of local communities who are often the closest guardians of historic sites. Jordanians involved in excavation, restoration, site management, and public awareness efforts have demonstrated their pride for the country's cultural heritage sites. A USAID-funded project from 2014 to 2024 assisted Jordanians in transforming artifacts from relics of the past into living connections to Jordan's identity and heritage. By harnessing Jordan's cultural heritage resources, local communities have created opportunities for education, employment, and economic development.

56

مشروع استدامة الإرث الثقافي بمشاركة المجتمعات المحلية

تُعد المجتمعات المحلية القريبة من المواقع الأثرية في طليعة الجهات المسؤولة عن الحفاظ على هذه المواقع والعناية بها. وبين عامي 2014 و2024، مولت الوكالة الأميركية للتنمية الدولية مشروعًا ممنهجًا يركز على دور المجتمع في الحفاظ، والإدارة المستدامة، والترويج لمصادر الإرث الثقافي في جميع أنحاء الأردن. وعمل المشروع مع شركاء محليين لتعزيز دور المجتمعات القريبة من المواقع الأثرية لاستثمار مواردها الثقافية في خلق فرص للتعليم، والتوظيف، والتنمية الاقتصادية.

57

Building a Rest House at Pella

(right, upper)
A rest house perched on a hillside overlooking the site of ancient Pella (modern Tabaqat Fahl) was completed in 1991 through support provided by USAID. The project engaged Jordanians who learned and employed traditional methods to build the structure designed by a noted Jordanian architect to harmonize with its surroundings. Visitors seated on its triple-arched patio can enjoy not only fresh food and drink but also an expansive vista of the ruins and the wider valley.

Supporting Ecotourism

(right, lower)
Established in 1989 and spanning over 115 square miles, the Dana Biosphere Reserve is Jordan's first and largest protected area. A stunning blend of diverse ecosystems, ranging from arid deserts to lush valleys, it is home to rare species, such as the Nubian ibex. USAID has played a key role in its ongoing conservation, partnering with the Royal Society for the Conservation of Nature to develop sustainable ecotourism, empower local Bedouin communities, and protect the reserve's rich biodiversity. These efforts help balance the needs of local populations with environmental preservation, turning Dana into a model of community-based conservation. Jordanians are generating income through eco-friendly activities such as guiding, handicrafts, and operating sustainable guesthouses, and building skills in conservation and environmental management.

بناء بيت استقبال في بيلا

(أقصى اليمين)
أنشئت عام 1991 استراحة على سفح يطل على موقع بيلا القديمة (طبقة فحل الحديثة) بتمويل من الوكالة الأميركية للتنمية الدولية. وشارك في المشروع أردنيون تعلموا أساليب تقليدية لبناء الاستراحة، والتي صممها مهندس معماري أردني بارز لتنسجم مع البيئة المحيطة. ويمكن للزوار الجلوس على الشرفة ذات الأقواس الثلاثة للاستمتاع بالطعام والشراب الطازجين، ومشهد فسيح يطل على الآثار والوادي المحيط.

دعم السياحة البيئية

(أدنى اليمين)
تأسست محمية ضانا للمحيط الحيوي عام 1989، على مساحة أكثر من 115 ميلًا مربعًا، وهي أول وأكبر منطقة محمية في الأردن. وتجمع المحمية بين مجموعة مذهلة من النظم البيئية المتنوعة، من الصحاري إلى الوديان الخضراء، وهي موطن لأنواع نادرة من الحيوانات، مثل الوعل النوبي. وساهمت الوكالة الأميركية للتنمية الدولية مساهمة رئيسة في الحفاظ المستمر عليها، من خلال الشراكة مع الجمعية الملكية لحماية الطبيعة، وذلك بتطوير السياحة البيئية المستدامة، وتمكين المجتمعات البدوية المحلية، وحماية التنوع البيولوجي الغني للمحمية. وتسهم هذه الجهود في تحقيق توازن بين احتياجات السكان المحليين والحفاظ على البيئة، ما جعل ضانا نموذجًا للحفاظ المجتمعي. ويحقق الأردنيون دخلًا ماليًا من خلال إقامة أنشطة صديقة للبيئة، مثل الإرشاد السياحي، والحرف اليدوية، وتشغيل بيوت الضيافة المستدامة، إلى جانب اكتساب مهارات في مجال الحفظ وإدارة البيئة.

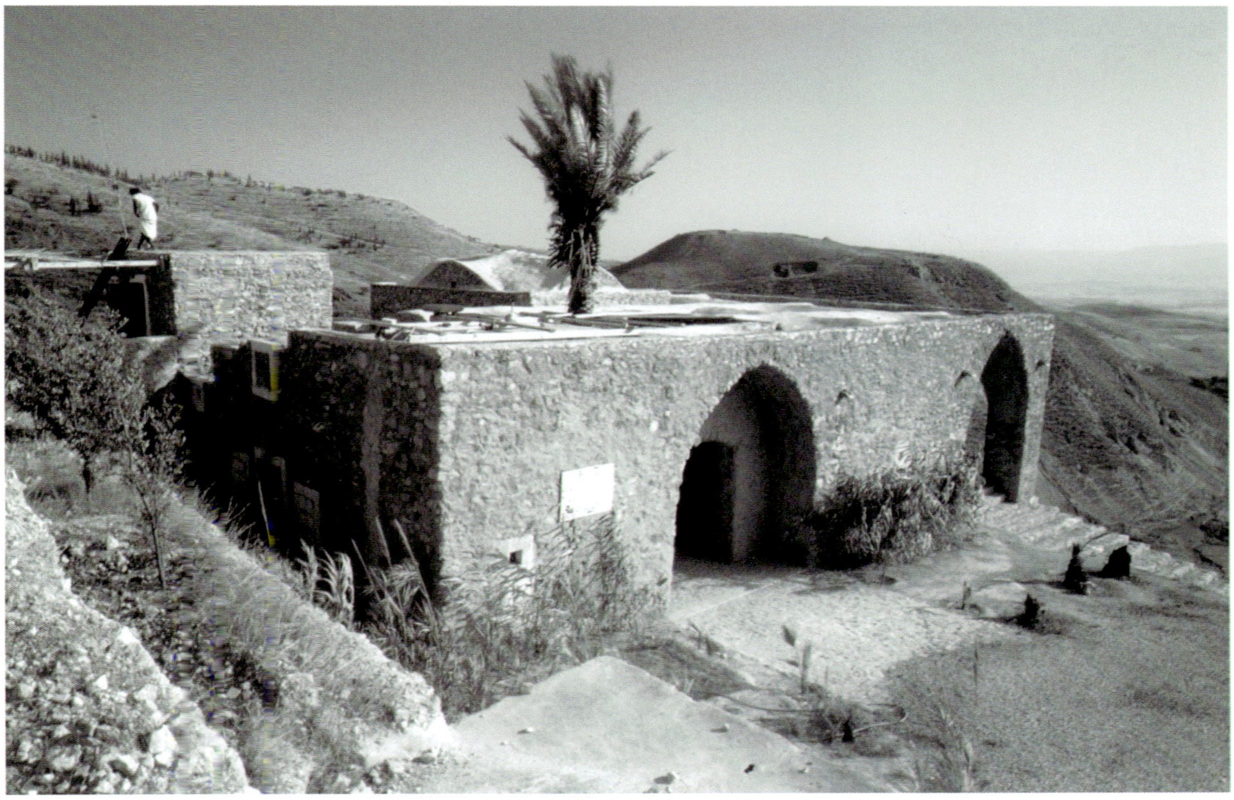

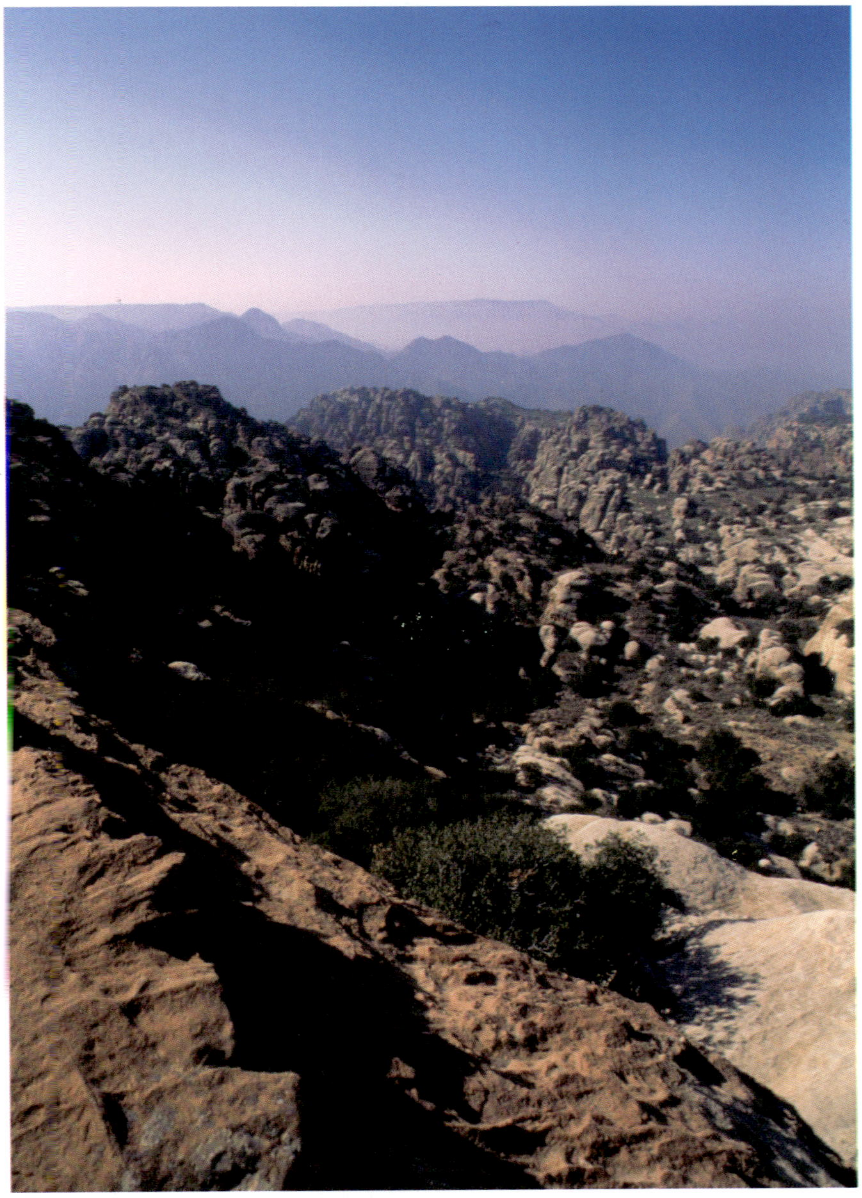

Revitalizing Water Management in Petra

إحياء نظام المياه في بترا

Iconic Petra is a marvel of ancient engineering and a testament to the ingenuity of the Nabateans. This UNESCO World Heritage site is renowned not only for its stunning rock-cut architecture but also for its sophisticated water management and flood-control systems of dams, cisterns, and channels to capture and store precious water. Beginning in 2017, the U.S. Department of State's Ambassador's Fund for Cultural Preservation coordinated with Jordanian partners on a project to restore the ancient Nabatean flood-control system. Through this initiative, researchers studied Petra's archaeology, environment, hydrology, and engineering with the goal of restoring the ancient terrace system that protected Petra from flash flooding and observing how it functioned between the 1st century BCE and the 4th century CE. The project has resulted in improvements of water management in Petra today, safeguarding this extraordinary archaeological site from erosion and flooding.

مدينة بترا أعجوبة في الهندسة القديمة وشهادة على براعة الأنباط. ولا يشتهر هذا الموقع المُدْرج على قائمة التراث العالمي لليونسكو بعمارته الصخرية المذهلة وحسب، بل أيضًا بأنظمة إدارة المياه ومكافحة الفيضانات المتطورة التي تشمل السدود، والخزانات، والقنوات التي تجمع المياه وتخزنها. وبدءًا من عام 2017، مول صندوق السفراء للحفاظ على التراث الثقافي مراحل متعددة من مشروع يهدف إلى استبناء نظام الأنباط القديم لمكافحة الفيضانات. ومن خلال هذه المبادرة، درس الباحثون آثار بترا وبيئتها، ونظامها المائي، وهندستها بهدف استبناء نظام المدرجات القديم الذي حمى بترا من الفيضانات المفاجئة، ودرسوا طريقة عمله بين القرن الأول قبل الميلاد والقرن الرابع الميلادي. وساهم المشروع في تحسين إدارة المياه في بترا اليوم، ما ساعد على حماية هذا الموقع الأثري الفريد من التآكل والفيضانات.

Conserving the Longest Tunnel of the Classical World

حماية أطول قناة في العالم الكلاسيكي

The Romans placed great importance on supplying their cities with water, and they developed sophisticated planning that enabled them to accomplish this wherever necessary throughout their empire. One such system, built in the 2nd century CE, allowed water to flow 105 miles from Syria to Jordan, with part of this ancient conduit preserved below the city of Gadara (modern Umm Qais). Conservation of a section of this tunnel—the longest tunnel known from Greco-Roman times—was made possible through support from the U.S. Department of State's Ambassador's Fund for Cultural Preservation and Jordan's Ministry of Tourism and Antiquities. Through meticulous restoration efforts in a remarkable feat of preservation work, the project not only stabilized the aqueduct's delicate structures but increased local and international interest in this significant archaeological site.

أولى الرومان أهمية كبيرة لتزويد مدنهم بالمياه، وطوروا خططًا معقدة مكنتهم من تحقيق ذلك في جميع أنحاء إمبراطوريتهم، حيث ما كان ذلك ضروريًا. ومن بين هذه الأنظمة، نظام مائي بني في القرن الثاني الميلادي، أتاح تدفق المياه لمسافة 105 أميال من سوريا إلى الأردن، وظل جزء من هذه القناة القديمة محفوظًا تحت مدينة جدارا (أم قيس الحديثة). ومول حفظَ هذا الجزء- وهو أطول نفق معروف من العصور اليونانية الرومانية- صندوق السفراء للحفاظ على التراث الثقافي بدعم من وزارة السياحة والآثار، وبذل فريق العمل جهود ترميم دقيقة تُعد إنجازًا مذهلًا في مجال الحفظ على الآثار. ولم يساهم المشروع في استقرار الهياكل الدقيقة للقناة فقط، بل زاد أيضًا من الاهتمام المحلي والدولي بهذا الموقع الأثري المهم.

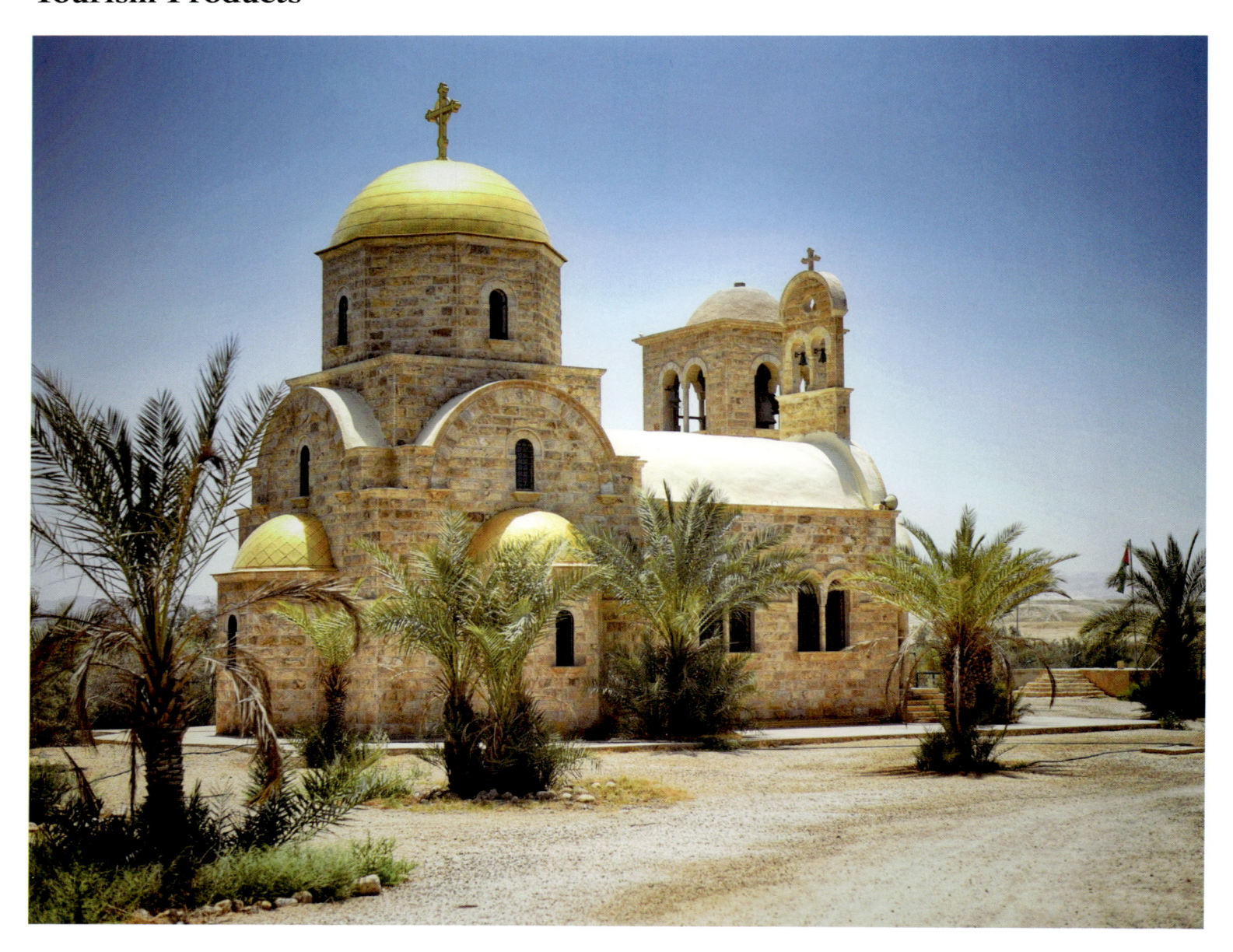

Developing and Diversifying Tourism Products

تعزيز المنتجات السياحية وتنويعها

From 2005 to 2014, USAID provided funding to help enhance Jordan's tourism sector by developing and diversifying tourism products, improving service quality, promoting sustainable tourism practices, and increasing international and domestic marketing efforts. Building local capacity was key. The project engaged local communities, fostered public-private partnerships, and encouraged environmentally and socially responsible tourism throughout the country, including at the Baptism Site (Bethany Beyond the Jordan). By diversifying Jordan's offerings and enhancing the standards, it contributed to an increase in tourist traffic, economic growth, and the preservation of the country's cultural and natural heritage.

من 2005 إلى 2014، قدمت الوكالة الأميركية للتنمية الدولية تمويلًا لتعزيز قطاع السياحة في الأردن من خلال تطوير المنتجات السياحية وتنويعها، وتحسين جودة الخدمات، وتعزيز ممارسات السياحة المستدامة، وزيادة جهود التسويق الدولية والمحلية. وأشرك المشروع المجتمعات المحلية في أعماله، وعزز الشراكات بين القطاعين العام والخاص، وشجع السياحة المسؤولة بيئيًا واجتماعيًا في جميع أنحاء البلاد، بما في ذلك في موقع المعمودية (بيت عنيا في الأردن). ومن خلال تحسين العروض والمعايير السياحية في الأردن، ساهم المشروع في زيادة حركة السائحين، وفي النمو الاقتصادي، والحفاظ على التراث الثقافي والطبيعي للبلاد.

62

Rebuilding Ancient Monuments

إعادة إحياء المعالم القديمة

Crowning one of the seven hills of Amman is the Citadel. Known in Arabic as Jabal al-Qal'a, it offers a panoramic view of Jordan's bustling capital city, and it is home to a wealth of archaeological treasures from the Iron Age and the Roman, Byzantine, and Umayyad eras. Projects supported by USAID and Jordanian partners in 1989 and 1990 embarked on an intricate exploration of the site's potential for preservation and public engagement and offered a roadmap for its future. By assessing both the historical significance and the logistical challenges of this iconic landmark, the study provided critical insights into enhancing its accessibility while protecting its archaeological integrity. This forward-thinking initiative laid the foundation for transforming the Citadel into a vibrant and beautiful cultural hub that speaks to Jordan's storied past.

تتربع قلعة عمان على واحدة من تلال عمان السبع، وتُعرف بالعربية باسم "جبل القلعة". وتتيح القلعة إطلالة بانورامية على العاصمة الأردنية النابضة بالحياة، وتحتضن ثروة من الكنوز الأثرية التي تعود إلى العصر الحديدي، والعصور الرومانية، والبيزنطية، والأموية. وبدعم من الوكالة الأميركية للتنمية الدولية والشركاء الأردنيين، بدأت في عامي 1989 و1990 مشاريع هدفت إلى استكشاف الإمكانيات الهائلة للموقع في مجالي الحفظ والتفاعل المجتمعي، ووضعت خريطة طريق لمستقبله. ومن خلال تقييم الأهمية التاريخية لهذا المعلم البارز وتحديد التحديات اللوجستية التي تواجهه، وفرت الدراسة رؤى مهمة لتعزيز وصول الزائرين إليه مع الحفاظ على سلامته الأثرية، فقد وضعت هذه المبادرة الاستشرافية الأساس لتحويل القلعة إلى مركز ثقافي حيوي وجميل يعبر عن الماضي العريق للأردن.

63

Conducting Emergency Excavations

الحفريات الطارئة

The U.S. National Endowment for the Humanities-supported emergency archaeological excavation at Wadi Fidan was a race against time to uncover the secrets of an ancient landscape before it succumbed to modern development. Nestled in the heart of southern Jordan, Wadi Fidan is a site of immense historical value, with evidence of prehistoric and early agricultural settlements, the Bronze Age, and the Iron Age. Swift yet meticulous excavation in 2003 revealed a wealth of artifacts and structural remnants, shedding light on early human activity and settlement patterns, technological development, and cultural heritage in southern Jordan.

دعمت المؤسسة الوطنية للعلوم الإنسانية التنقيبات الأثرية الطارئة التي أُجريت في وادي فيدان، فدخلت في سباق ضد الزمن للكشف عن أسرار مشهد تاريخي قديم قبل أن يندثر تحت وطأة التطور الحديث. ويقع وادي فيدان في قلب جنوب الأردن، وهو موقع ذو قيمة تاريخية هائلة، إذ يحتوي على أدلة على المستقرات الزراعية الأولى، وعلى العصرين البرونزي والحديدي. وفي عام 2003، كشفت التنقيبات السريعة والدقيقة، في الوقت نفسه، عن ثروة من القطع الأثرية وبقايا المباني، ما ألقى الضوء على النشاط البشري المبكر في الموقع، وأنماط الاستقرار فيه، وعلى التطور التكنولوجي، وعلى التراث الثقافي في جنوب الأردن.

Restoring the Qasr Al-Muwaqqar Reservoir

ترميم خزَّان الموقر الصحراوي

Very little remains of the Umayyad-period desert castle (qasr) at Al-Muwaqqar, on the outskirts of Amman. Yet its reservoir, which Caliph Yazid II ordered built in 722–723 CE, is in use today thanks to restoration in 1952 to facilitate use of modern agricultural techniques. Funding was provided under the U.S. Point Four Program, established by President Harry Truman in 1949. The updates to the reservoir likely represent the first restoration of an ancient site in Jordan conducted jointly by the United States and the Hashemite Kingdom of Jordan.

لم يتبق سوى القليل من قصر الموقر الصحراوي الواقع على أطراف عمان، والذي يعود إلى العصر الأموي. ا ومع ذلك، فإن خزان الماء التابع له، والذي أمر ببنائه الخليفة يزيد الثاني في عامَي 722-723 ميلادي، لا يزال قيد الاستخدام اليوم بفضل أعمال الترميم التي تمّت في عام 1952 لدعم استخدام التقنيات الزراعية الحديثة، والممولة من برنامج النقطة الرابعة الذي أطلقه الرئيس هاري ترومان في عام 1949. وتُعَدُّ هذه التحديثات للخزان على الأرجح أول عملية ترميم لموقع أثري في الأردن نُفذت بشكل مشترك بين الولايات المتحدة والمملكة الأردنية الهاشمية.

Improving the Tourism Experience

تحسين التجربة السياحية

In 2015, USAID funded a pioneering effort to preserve and revitalize Bir Madhkur, an ancient and important trading hub in southern Jordan, most notable for its Roman/Byzantine fort. The joint U.S.-Jordanian efforts, which also received support from the International Union for Conservation of Nature and other partners, revitalized the trails that link Bir Madhkur to Petra, installed interpretive panels along the route, and combated erosion and other forms of degradation by building terraced walkways to limit foot traffic in risk-susceptible areas.

في عام 2015، مولت الوكالة الأميركية للتنمية الدولية جهودًا رائدة للحفاظ على موقع بير مدكور في جنوب الأردن وإحيائه، وهو مركز تجاري قديم ذو أهمية كبيرة، ويُعرف بشكل خاص بحصنه الروماني/البيزنطي. وأسفرت الجهود المشتركة بين الولايات المتحدة والأردن، والتي حظيت أيضًا بدعم من الاتحاد الدولي لحماية الطبيعة وشركاء آخرين، عن إعادة إحياء المسارات التي تربط بير مدكور ببترا، وتركيب لوحات تفسيرية على طول الطريق. كما تضمنت المبادرة مكافحة التآكل وأشكال التدهور الأخرى على طول المسار، من خلال بناء مسارات مدرَّجة للتقليل من حركة السير في المناطق الخطرة.

Building Local Capacity in Rural Jordan

From 2003 to 2008, USAID, the Council of American Overseas Research Centers, and several private foundations supported excavation of an ancient elite residence at Beidha, a suburb of Petra, notable for its ornate column capitals adorned with heads of Greco-Roman deities and other divine and semi-divine beings such as Ampelos, the personification of the grapevine and companion of Dionysus, god of wine. The excavations and associated training helped develop local capacity for and enhanced understanding of the site to promote tourism development in and around Beidha.

تنمية القدرات المحلية في الريف الأردني

من 2003 إلى 2008، دعمت الوكالة الأميركية للتنمية الدولية، ومجلس مراكز البحوث الأميركية الخارجية، وعدد من المؤسسات الخاصة عمليات التنقيب في مسكن قديم فخم في بيضا، إحدى ضواحي بترا، يتميز برؤوس أعمدة مزخرفة تحمل رؤوس آلهة يونانية رومانية، وكائنات إلهية، وأنصاف آلهة أخر، مثل أمبيلوس، الذي يجسِّد كرمة العنب ورفيق ديونيسوس، إله النبيذ. وساعدت عمليات التنقيب والتدريب المرتبط بها في تطوير القدرات البشرية المحلية وزيادة فهمنا للموقع، ما ساهم في تطوير السياحة في البيضا والمناطق المحيطة بها.

Revitalizing Madaba

(following pages)
The city of Madaba underwent a major development project initiated in 2006 with support from USAID and in close cooperation with Jordan's Ministry of Tourism and Antiquities. Intended to lengthen visitors' stays in one of Jordan's top tourist destinations, the project focused on Madaba's history as a center of mosaic production and on its religious heritage. Visitors and residents alike have benefited from improvements to Madaba's charming streets and shops, interpretive signs at its historical locations, and support for traditional crafts, restaurants, and other local enterprises. From 2015 to 2023, the U.S. Department of State supported a project through which American, Jordanian, and Italian teams are seeking to establish a state-of-the-art museum in Madaba's historic downtown.

تطوير مدينة مادبا

(يتبع في الصفحات التالية)
في عام 2006، شهدت مدينة مادبا مشروع تطوير كبيرًا بتمويل من الوكالة الأميركية للتنمية الدولية، بالتعاون الوثيق مع وزارة السياحة والآثار، ودائرة الآثار العامة. وهدف المشروع إلى زيادة مدة إقامة الزوار في واحدة من أبرز الوجهات السياحية في الأردن، مع التركيز على مادبا كمركز لإنتاج الفسيفساء وعلى تراثها الديني. واستفاد الزوار والمقيمون على حد سواء من التحسينات في شوارع المدينة الساحرة ومحلاتها التجارية، بالإضافة إلى اللوحات التفسيرية في المواقع التاريخية، فضلًا عن الدعم المقدم للحرف التقليدية، والمطاعم، والمؤسسات الأخرى. ومن 2015 إلى 2023، دعم صندوق السفراء للحفاظ على التراث الثقافي ومنحة تطوير الشراكة التابعة للسفارة الأميركية مشروعًا سعت فيه فرق أميركية، وأردنية، وإيطالية إلى إنشاء متحف حديث في وسط المدينة التاريخي.

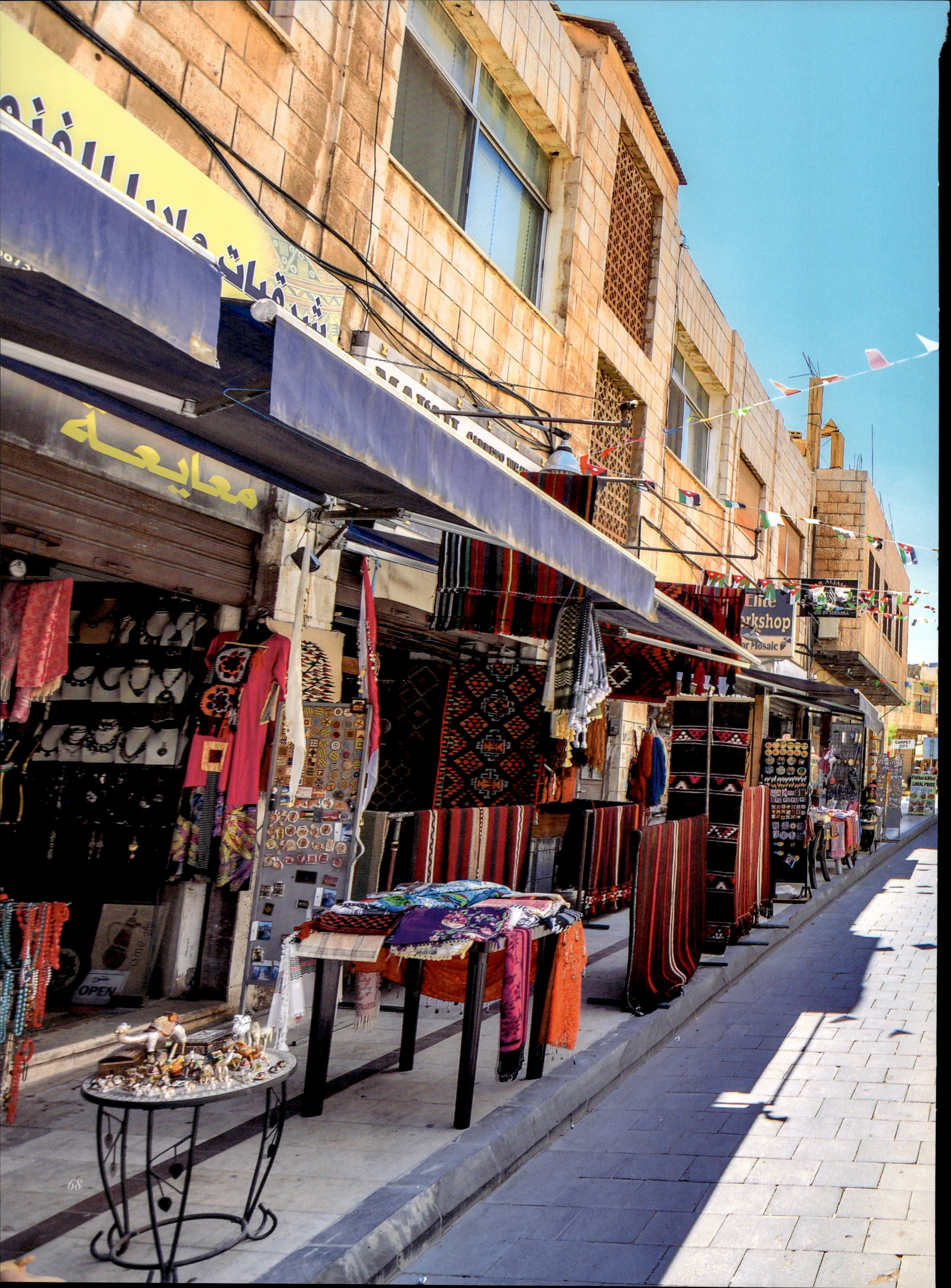
OPEN

وزارة السياحة والآثار / مديرية سياحة مادبا
يهنئون قائد الوطن المفدى
بمناسبة عيد الاستقلال ويوم الجيش
Independence Day

Building Economic Sustainability through Tourism

USAID funded a project dedicated to enhancing the competitiveness and sustainability of Jordan's tourism sector in order to drive economic growth, create jobs, and improve community livelihoods. Running from 2015 to 2019, it focused on market diversification, product development, human-resource training, public-private partnerships, sustainable tourism practices, and community engagement. Supporting experiential and adventure tourism helped to diversify the sector. By promoting Jordan's diverse attractions and encouraging a deeper engagement with the local landscapes and environment, this project contributed to the growth and resilience of the country's tourism industry.

تحقيق الاستدامة الاقتصادية من خلال السياحة

مولت الوكالة الأميركية للتنمية الدولية مشروعًا لتعزيز تنافسية قطاع السياحة في الأردن واستدامته، بهدف تعزيز النمو الاقتصادي، وخلق فرص العمل، وتحسين سبل العيش المجتمعية. واستمر المشروع من عام 2015 إلى 2019، وركز على تنويع الأسواق، وتطوير المنتجات، وتدريب الموارد البشرية، والشراكات بين القطاعين العام والخاص، وممارسات السياحة المستدامة، والمشاركة المجتمعية. ومن خلال الترويج لمختلف معالم الأردن السياحية وضمان استفادة المجتمعات المحلية من ذلك، ساهم المشروع في نمو صناعة السياحة في البلاد واستدامتها.

Documenting the History of the Deserts

توثيق تاريخ الصحراء

Through meticulous surveying and state-of-the-art digital documentation, a project in 2022 supported by USAID recorded 5,609 ancient rock inscriptions, petroglyphs, historic structures, and unique cultural and geological elements in the spectacular Wadi Rum Protected Area. The resulting database has helped monitor and preserve the desert's breathtaking landscape and cultural remains and has created a valuable reference tool for scholars and researchers. The work has captured the essence of Jordan's most iconic desert landscapes, which passersby and inhabitants have crossed for millennia, leaving behind traces that tell stories of life and travel in this harsh and beautiful environment.

من خلال المسح الدقيق والتوثيق الرقمي المتقدم، سُجل في مشروع أُجري عام 2022 بدعم من الوكالة الأميركية للتنمية الدولي 5609 نقشًا صخريًا قديمًا، ورسومًا صخرية، ومعالم تاريخية، وعناصر ثقافية وجيولوجية فريدة في محمية وادي رم الطبيعية. وساعدت قاعدة البيانات الناتجة في مراقبة وحفظ المشاهد الطبيعية المدهشة، والمواقع الثقافية في الصحراء، ووفرت أداة مرجعية قيِّمة للباحثين والعلماء. وقد التقطت هذه الأعمال جوهر المشاهد الصحراوية الأكثر شهرة في الأردن، والتي عبَرها المارة والسكان على مر العصور، تاركين وراءهم آثارًا تروي قصص الحياة والسَفر في هذه البيئة القاسية والجميلة.

Conveying the Stories of the Holy Sites of Jordan

سرد قصص المواقع المقدسة في الأردن

In 1996, USAID funded the publication of an essential book, *The Holy Sites of Jordan*. The first comprehensive work on the subject, it includes Islamic and Christian sites with English and Arabic captions, which made these sites accessible to more people than ever before. Among the book's entries is the so-called Tomb of Aaron, a Mamluk-era Muslim shrine built atop Jabal Harun (the "Mountain of Aaron") in Petra to honor the brother of Moses.

في عام 1996، مولت الوكالة الأمريكية للتنمية الدولية نشر كتاب مهم عنوانه "المواقع المقدسة في الأردن". وهو أول عمل شامل في هذا الموضوع، يشمل المواقع الإسلامية والمسيحية مع شروحات للصور باللغتين الإنجليزية والعربية، فقرَّب الكتاب هذه المواقع للناس أكثر من أي وقت مضى. ومن بين هذه المواقع الموقع المسمى مقام هارون، وهو ضريح إسلامي من العصر المملوكي بُني على قمة جبل هارون في بترا تكريمًا لشقيق النبي موسى.

Expanding Destination Tourism

تعزيز سياحة الوجهات

Located 15 miles northwest of Amman, the city of As-Salt is inscribed in the UNESCO World Heritage List for its history as a place of tolerance and urban hospitality. In 2017, USAID, in coordination with Jordanian partners, developed a plan to enhance tourism products and services in the city. Implemented from 2018–2020, the plan detailed strategies to attract new visitors, upgrade visitor amenities, create an image for the city based on its heritage (including its traditional system of guest houses), and showcase the city's importance during the dawn of Hashemite rule in the 1920s.

تقع مدينة السلط على بُعد 15 ميلًا شمال غرب عمان، وهي مسجلة في قائمة التراث العالمي لليونسكو بفضل تاريخها كمكان للتسامح والضيافة الحضرية. وفي عام 2017، مولت الوكالة الأميركية للتنمية الدولية وضع خطة لتعزيز منتجات وخدمات السياحة في المدينة، والتي نُفذت من عام 2018 إلى 2020، وتضمنت إستراتيجياتٍ لجذب الزوار الجدد، وتحسين مرافق الزوار، وخلق طابع للمدينة ينبع من تراثها - بما في ذلك نظام المضافات التقليدية فيها - إلى جانب الضيافة الحديثة، مع تسليط الضوء على أهميتها في الفترة الهاشمية المبكرة، في عشرينات القرن الماضي.

Exploring the Unknown

استكشاف المجهول

In the vast eastern lands of Jordan, the Wadi Bayir stretches more than 50 miles. In 1981 and 1982, the U.S. National Endowment for the Humanities supported a comprehensive survey of this rarely studied region. The work explored the area's prehistoric significance and facilitated discovery of inscriptions and artifacts that continue to define scholars' understanding of the area today. Bayir's importance is most evident through the presence of its wells, which caravans and other travelers relied on as they passed through this stark, arid region.

في أراضي الأردن الشرقية الفسيحة، يمتد وادي باير لأكثر من 50 ميلًا. وفي عامي 1981 و1982، دعمت المؤسسة الوطنية للإنسانيات مسحًا شاملًا لهذه المنطقة التي نادرًا ما تمت دراستها. واستكشفت الأعمال أهمية المنطقة في فترات ما قبل التاريخ وفي الفترات التاريخية، مع التركيز على اكتشاف النقوش واللقى الأثرية، والتي لا تزال تميز هذه المنطقة اليوم. وتكمن أهمية باير بشكل خاص بآبارها التي اعتمدت عليها القوافل وسواها من المسافرين أثناء عبورهم لهذه المنطقة القاحلة الوعرة.

Saving Ancient History in Urban Environments

إنقاذ التاريخ القديم في البيئات الحضرية

The excavation and restoration of the Byzantine church at the Amman Citadel, undertaken to preserve its architectural and historical significance, received USAID support from 1990 to 1993. Restoration efforts revealed mosaics, columns, and other structural elements that showcase the artistry and craftsmanship of the period. Today the site, which offers splendid views of the city below, serves as a significant cultural and historical landmark, and offers a glimpse of the rich cultural heritage of Amman.

تلقت أعمال التنقيب والترميم للكنيسة البيزنطية في جبل القلعة بعمان، والتي أُجريت للحفاظ على أهميتها المعمارية والتاريخية، دعمًا من الوكالة الأميركية للتنمية الدولية من عام 1990 إلى 1993. وكشفت جهود الترميم عن فسيفساء، وأعمدة، وعناصر معمارية أخرى، ما أبرز فنون تلك الفترة وحرفيتها. ويعد الموقع اليوم، والذي يوفر إطلالات رائعة على المدينة تحته، معلمًا ثقافيًا وتاريخيًا مهمًا، ونافذة على التراث الغني لعمان.

75

Supporting Significant Publications

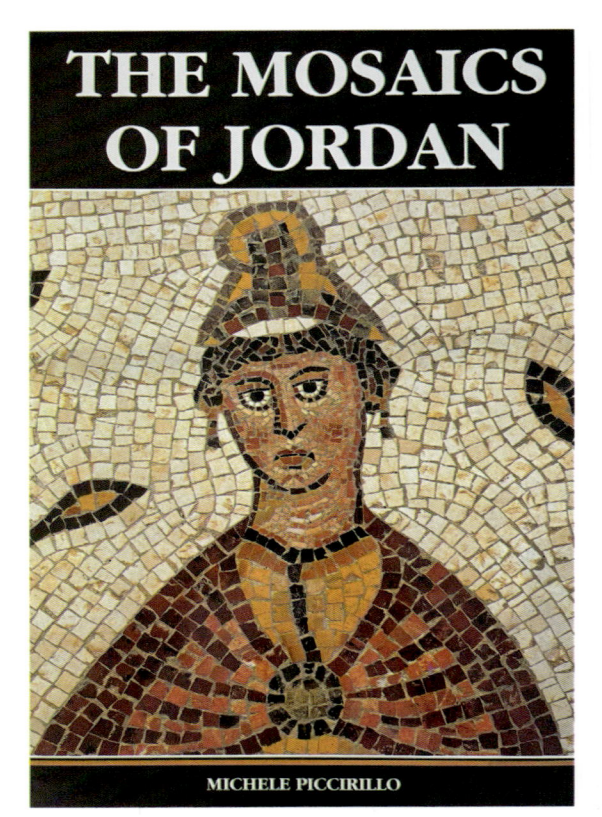

دعم المنشورات المهمة

The Mosaics of Jordan by Michele Piccirillo, supported by USAID in 1993, is a groundbreaking exploration of Jordan's rich mosaic heritage, showcasing the intricate artistry and cultural significance of these ancient artworks. Through stunning photographs and scholarly insights in the book, it highlights the historical and artistic context of Jordan's then most renowned mosaics, most of which date back to the Roman and Byzantine periods. This publication serves as both an invaluable resource for scholars and a visual journey into the enduring legacy of Jordan's artistic traditions.

يُعد كتاب "فسيفساء الأردن" للمؤلف ميشيل بتشيريلو، والذي دعمته الوكالة الأميركية للتنمية الدولية في عام 1993، استكشافًا رائدًا لتراث الأردن الغني من الفسيفساء، إذ يعرض براعة هذا الفن ويبرز الأهمية الثقافية لهذه الأعمال الفنية القديمة. وتبين الصور المدهشة والرؤى العلمية في الكتاب السياق التاريخي والفني لأشهر قطع الفسيفساء في الأردن، والتي يعود معظمها إلى الفترات الرومانية والبيزنطية. ويُعد هذا الكتاب مصدرًا لا غنى عنه للباحثين، ورحلة بصرية في إرث الأردن الفني المستمر.

Restoring Religiously Significant Sites

ترميم المواقع ذات الأهمية الدينية

Perched in the rugged hills of southern Jordan, the Sanctuary of Lot at Deir 'Ain 'Abata is believed to be the place where the prophet Lot sought refuge while fleeing the destruction of Sodom and Gomorrah. The excavation and preservation of the Sanctuary of Lot, supported by USAID in 1995, offers visitors a glimpse of the ancient rock-cut chambers and landscapes of early Christian and Islamic eras in Jordan.

يقع كهف لوط بدير عين عباطة في التلال الوعرة بجنوب الأردن. ويُعتقد أن هذا الموقع المقدس هو المكان الذي لجأ إليه النبي لوط أثناء هروبه من دمار سدوم وعمورة. ودعمت الوكالة الأميركية للتنمية الدولية في عام 1995 أعمال التنقيب والصيانة في كهف لوط، ما وفر للزوار فرصة للاطلاع على الغرف المنحوتة في الصخور والمشاهد الطبيعية التي تعكس تاريخ المسيحية المبكرة والعصر الإسلامي في الأردن.

Exploring Jordan's Southern Reaches

استكشاف الجنوب الأردني

From the remote and parched southern plains emerged a once thriving ancient settlement at Humayma. In 1982, the U.S. National Endowment for the Humanities (NEH) sponsored an archaeological project that began to scratch the surface of what is now known to be a long and rich history. Situated at the crossroads of ancient trade routes, Humayma flourished under Nabataean, Roman, and early Islamic influences. The NEH-funded excavation revealed an impressive array of artifacts, structures, and inscriptions that provided invaluable insights into the area's cultural and economic exchanges over centuries and the broader historical context of the ancient Near East. The excavation was pivotal in furthering the preservation of the site and fostering international collaboration in archaeological research, ensuring that Humayma's complex past continues to inform both academic study and public appreciation of Jordan's rich heritage.

من السهول الجنوبية القاحلة والنائية ازدهرت ذات يوم في موقع الحميمة مستوطنة قديمة. وفي عام 1982، مولت المؤسسة الوطنية للعلوم الإنسانية مشروعًا أثريًا بدأ بالكشف عن معلومات تاريخية أولية، حتى بتنا نعرف اليوم أنه كان تاريخًا طويلًا وغنيًا. وتقع الحميمة عند ملتقى طرق تجارية قديمة، وازدهرت في فترات الأنباط، والرومان، وفي العصور الإسلامية المبكرة. وكشفت التنقيبات الممولة من المؤسسة عن مجموعة مثيرة للإعجاب من القطع الأثرية، والمنشآت، والنقوش التي قدمت رؤى قيِّمة عن التبادلات الثقافية والاقتصادية التي سادت المنطقة على مدى قرون، حيث أضافت كل حقبة طبقات تعين على فهم دور المنطقة في السياق التاريخي الأوسع للشرق الأدنى القديم. وكان دعم المؤسسة لهذه التنقيبات محوريًا في تعزيز الحفاظ على الموقع وتشجيع التعاون الدولي في البحث الأثري، ما يكفل استمرار الماضي الغني للحميمة في إثراء الدراسة الأكاديمية ويكفل تقدير الجمهور للتراث الغني للأردن.

Strengthening Community Ties to Heritage Sites

تعزيز الروابط المجتمعية مع المواقع الأثرية

In 2018, USAID coordinated with Jordanian partners to launch a program of educational workshops, field trips, and activities to strengthen community bonds to heritage sites. The program emphasized early education to counteract vandalism and misinformation about heritage sites, promoting a sense of ownership and stewardship throughout Jordan, especially among youth. Through this initiative, Jordanians connected more deeply with their cultural heritage and celebrated Jordan's cultural legacy.

في عام 2018، نسقت الوكالة الأميركية للتنمية الدولية مع شركاء أردنيين لإطلاق برنامج طُوِّر لتوحيد وتعزيز الروابط المجتمعية بالمواقع الأثرية، من خلال ورش عمل تعليمية، ورحلات ميدانية، وفعاليات مشوقة. وركز البرنامج على التعليم المبكر لمكافحة تخريب المواقع الأثرية، ولتبديد المعلومات المضللة عنها، وتعزيز شعور الناس بملكيتهم لهذه المواقع ورعايتها في جميع أنحاء الأردن، خاصة بين الأجيال الشابة. ومن خلال هذه المبادرة، تعمق ارتباط الأردنيين بتراثهم الثقافي، واحتفوا بالإرث الثقافي الغني للأردن.

Navigating Ancient Roads and Settlements

البحث في الطرق والمستقرات القديمة

In ancient times, a road known today as the Via Nova Traiana extended between the Red Sea port of Aqaba and Bostra (modern Bosra) in Syria. It was built by the Romans in the early 2nd century CE over the remains of more ancient trails not long after they annexed the Nabataean kingdom in 106 CE. The road facilitated the movement of commerce, communications, and the military, a hallmark of Roman expansion. One of its best-preserved sections occurs in southern Jordan at Tuwaneh, where the United States Information Agency supported a survey of the associated archaeological remains in 1992. The survey provided insights into settlement patterns, architecture, and material culture during the Roman period.

في العصور القديمة، كان هناك طريق عُرف اليوم باسم "طريق تراجان الجديدة" تمتد من ميناء العقبة على البحر الأحمر إلى بُصرى (الشام) في سوريا. وكان الرومان بنوا هذه الطريق في أوائل القرن الثاني الميلادي فوق بقايا مسارات قديمة، بعد فترة قصيرة من ضمهم للمملكة النبطية في عام 106 ميلادي. وسهلت الطريق حركة التجارة، والاتصالات، والجيوش التي تميز بها التوسع الروماني. ويقع أحد أفضل أقسامها المحفوظة بجنوب الأردن، في خربة التوانة، حيث استكشف مسح مدعوم من الوكالة الأميركية للتنمية الدولية بقايا الطريق الأثرية في عام 1992، فعرفنا منه أنماط الاستقرار، والعمارة، والثقافة المادية خلال الفترة الرومانية.

Supporting Research at the Cradle of American Archaeology in Jordan

دعم البحث العلمي في مهد علم الآثار الأميركي في الأردن

The Tall Hisban excavation, which began in 1968, is one of the premier locations for study of the history and daily life of the Mamluk era. Over the decades, Tall Hisban, with its associated excavations and field school based at Andrews University in Michigan, has received support from the U.S. National Endowment for the Humanities (1977, 1978, 1980, 2008) and the U.S. Department of State's Ambassador's Fund for Cultural Preservation (2005). The site is iconic in Jordanian archaeology, and Tall Hisban has served as a type site for dating archaeological periods in Jordan spanning thousands of years. Additionally, three generations of Jordanian and foreign archaeologists have trained at Tall Hisban, and local community members have long been involved in excavations. The project has also been pivotal in developing the field of Islamic archaeology and demonstrating how archaeology can enhance understanding of imperial interventions.

تلقى العمل الأثري الطويل الأمد في تل حسبان، والذي بدأ في عام 1968، والتنقيبات، والمدرسة الميدانية المرتبطة بها التي تتولاها جامعة أندروز في ميشغان، دعمًا من الهيئة الوطنية للفنون والإنسانيات في سنوات 1977، 1978، 1980، و2008، ومن صندوق الحفاظ على التراث الثقافي في عام 2005. ويُعد تل حسبان أيقونة في علم الآثار الأردني، وقد تدربت فيه ثلاثة أجيال من علماء الآثار الأردنيين والأجانب، مع إيلاء الأولوية للمشاركة المجتمعية. ويُتخذ التل موقعًا مرجعيًا لتأريخ الفترات الأثرية في الأردن التي تمتد لآلاف السنين. وأدخلَ الباحثون في التل المناهج العلمية لما يسمى "علم الآثار الجديد" (أو علم الآثار الإجرائي) إلى الأردن، مع التركيز على دراسة أنماط الإنتاج الثقافي والتغيير الطويل الأمد. كما كان المشروع محوريًا في تطوير علم الآثار الإسلامي، وفي إبراز دور علم الآثار في تبيان أثر القوى الإقليمية والعظمى على المواقع المحلية.

81

Granting Fellowships to Experience Jordan

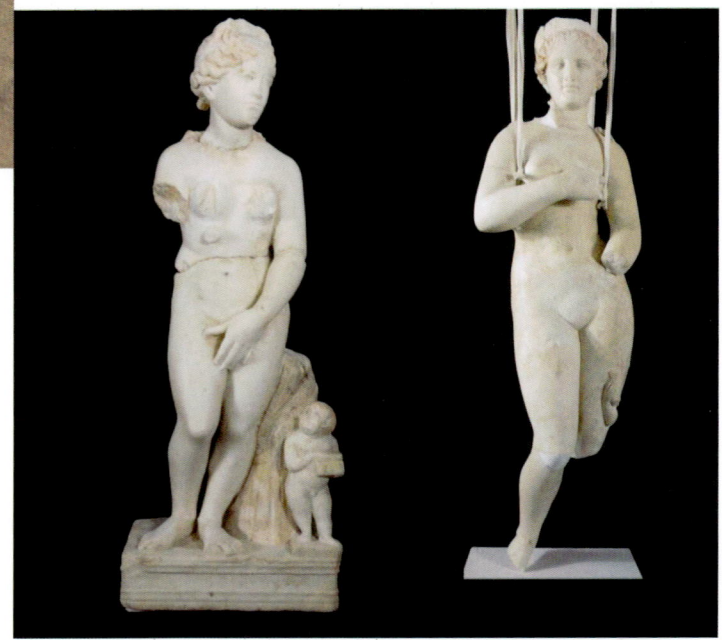

منح زمالات للأردن للتجربة

Since 1970, more than 1,000 Americans have been awarded teaching, research, and educational fellowships to Jordan through the United States Information Agency, the U.S. Department of State, the Near and Middle East Research and Training Act (NMERTA), and the U.S. National Endowment for the Humanities. These fellows, hailing from diverse professional backgrounds, typically reside in Jordan, immersing themselves in the country's rich culture and exchanging ideas with peers. One example is the recipient of a 2018 postdoctoral fellowship to conserve two marble statues of Aphrodite that had been found in Petra not long before with some of their paint remarkably still intact. These objects, which were the focus of an international workshop held in Amman in 2023, provide new evidence for the importation of marble and production of marble statuary, the adoption of Greco-Roman practices, and the domestic display of statuary.

منذ عام 1970، مُنح أكثر من 1000 أميركي زمالات دراسية، وبحثية، وتعليمية من خلال وكالة المعلومات الأميركية، ووزارة الخارجية، والصندوق الوطني الأميركي للبحث والتدريب الأثري، والهيئة الوطنية للفنون والعلوم الإنسانية. ويقيم هؤلاء المبعوثون الذين ينتمون إلى خلفيات مهنية متنوعة، عادة، في الأردن، وينغمسون في ثقافة البلاد الثرية، ويتبادلون الأفكار مع أقرانهم. وأحد الأمثلة على ذلك هو الآثاري المستقل الذي حصل في عام 2018 على منحة ما بعد الدكتوراة لترميم تمثالين من الرخام لأفروديت، عُثر عليهما في بترا قبل ذلك بفترة وجيزة، ولا يزال بعض طلائهما محفوظًا بشكل ملحوظ. وكانت هذه التماثيل محور ورشة عمل دولية عُقدت في عمّان عام 2023، قُدمت فيها أدلة جديدة على استيراد الرخام وإنتاج التماثيل الرخامية، وعلى تبني الممارسات الإغريقية والرومانية، وعرض التماثيل في المنازل.

Chronicling Rock Art and Epigraphy in Wadi Rum

تأريخ الفنون الصخرية والكتابات في وادي رم

(and following pages)
For millennia the deserts of Wadi Rum and its canyon walls have provided a magnificent canvas for the intrepid Bedouins and other travelers who have dared to cross its shifting sands. The societies who have thrived in these deserts left records of their life and ways, etched into the rocks. From 2016 to 2019, USAID funded the documentation of rock art and inscriptions in Wadi Rum using photography and 3-D scanning. The project demonstrated the historical significance of these cultural remains and ensured that they are preserved for future generations.

(يتبع في الصفحات التالية)
لآلاف السنين قدمت صحاري وادي رم وجدرانه الصخرية لوحة رائعة للبدو الشجعان وغيرهم من المسافرين الذين عبروا رمالها المتحركة، فقد خلَّفت المجتمعات التي ازدهرت في هذه الصحاري سجلات لحياتها وطرقها محفورة في الصخور. ومن 2016 إلى 2019، مولت الوكالة الأميركية للتنمية الدولية مشروعًا لتوثيق الفن الصخري والنقوش في وادي رم باستخدام التصوير الفوتوغرافي والمسح الثلاثي الأبعاد. وأظهر المشروع الأهمية التاريخية لهذه الآثار الثقافية وضمِن الحفاظ عليها للأجيال القادمة.

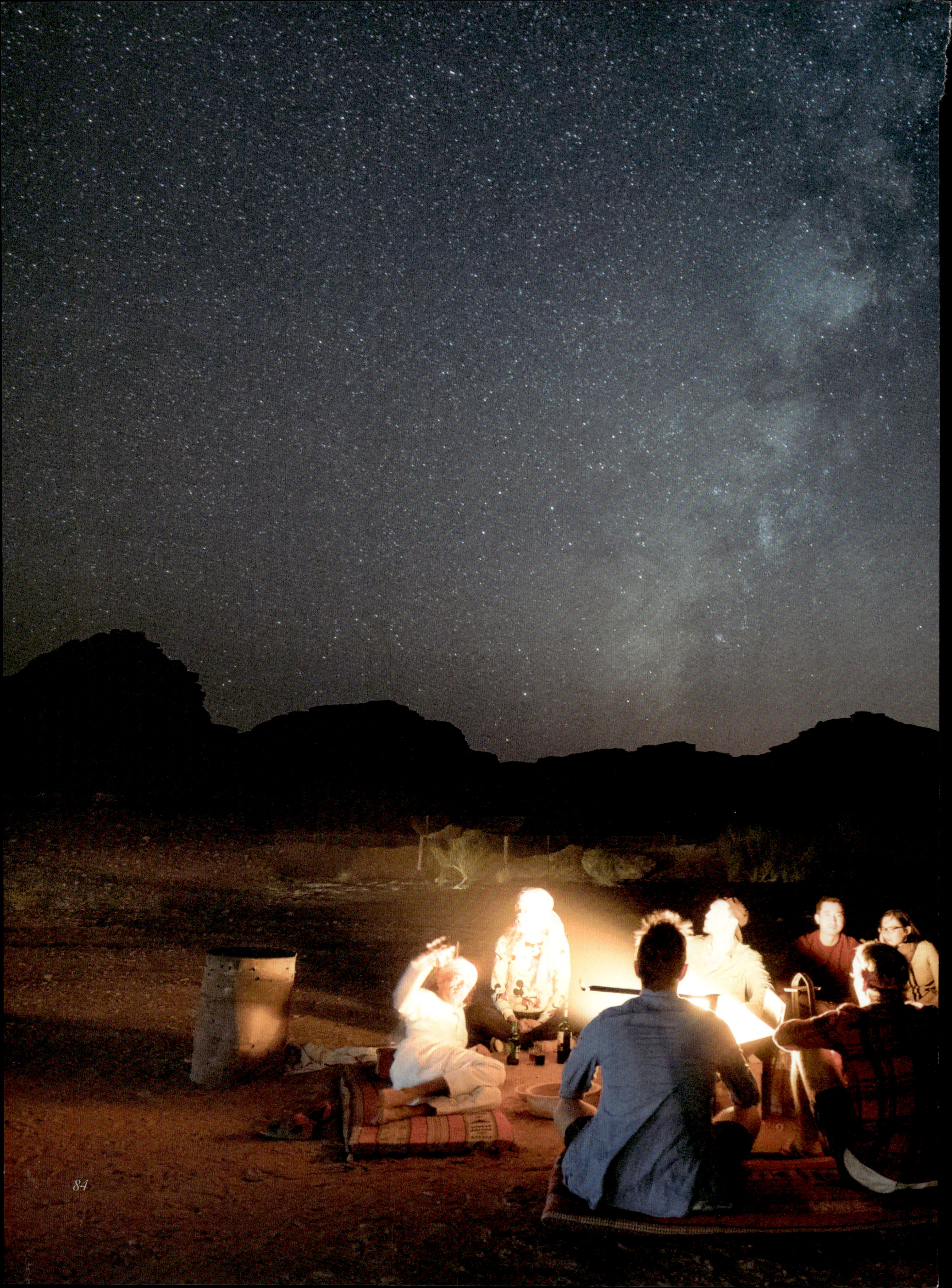

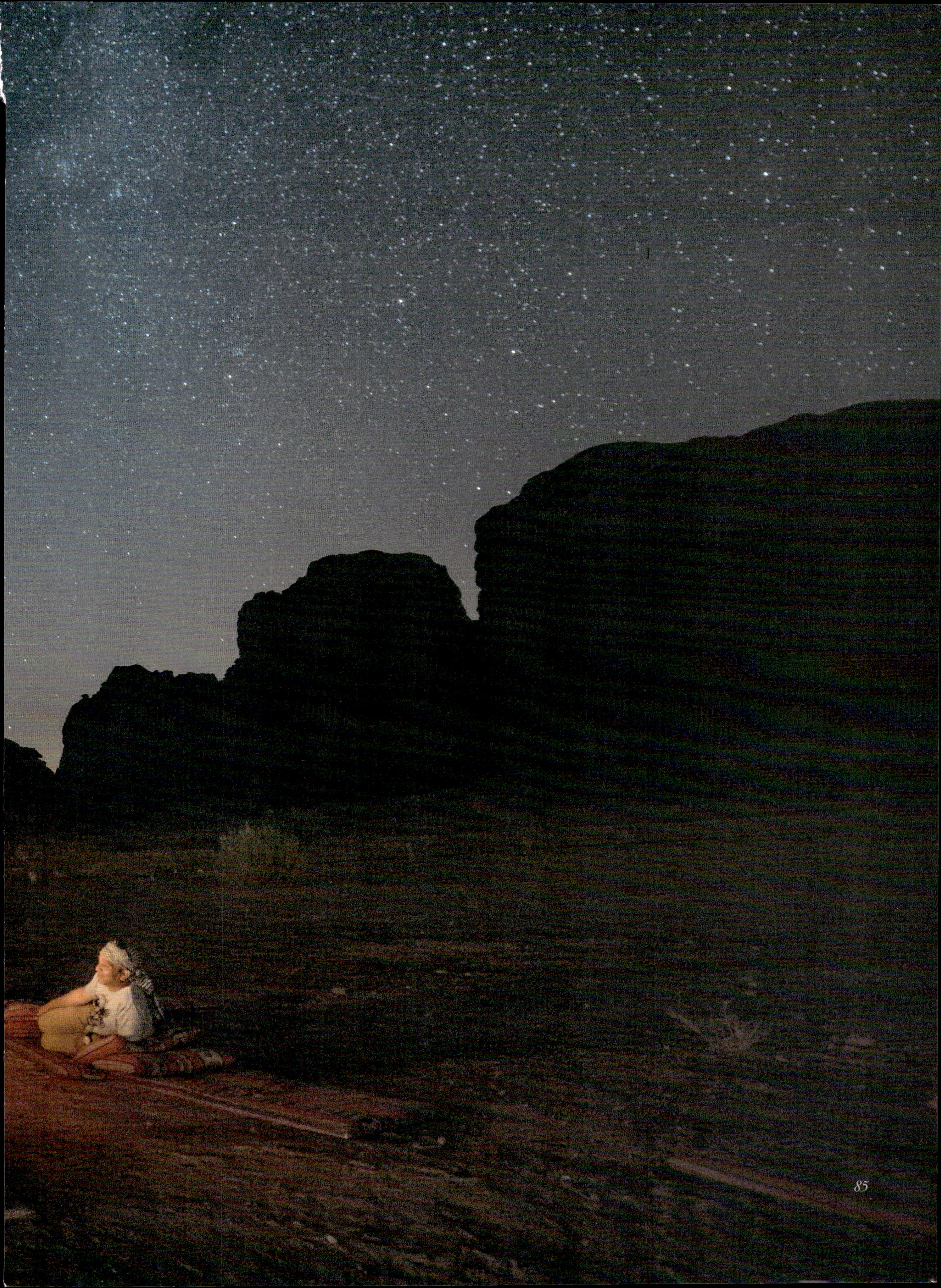

Photo Captions and Credits

1. **Establishing National Parks (p. 2):** A column capital of the Treasury in Petra being lifted back into place in the early 1960s. *(Photo courtesy of the Jordan Tourism Board.)*

2. **Developing Bethany Beyond the Jordan (p. 3):** The natural spring thought to be where John the Baptist baptized Jesus Christ. The Baptism Site business plan was developed by Chemonics International, Inc., through the USAID-funded Jordan Tourism Development Project (Siyaha). United States government funding has contributed to other site improvements as well. *(Photo courtesy of the Jordan Tourism Board.)*

3. **Revealing Roman Petra (p. 4):** The Roman-era colonnaded street in Petra. A project was undertaken here by the American Center of Research in the 1990s, with various aspects by Zbigniew T. Fiema, Chrysanthos Kanellopoulos, Ueli Bellwald, Hassan Safarini, Pierre Bikai, and Dakhillallah Qublan. *(Photo from the Jane Taylor collection, ACOR Digital Archive.)*

4. **Supporting Petra (pp. 5–7):** Page 5: Ancient rock dam built by the Nabataeans for water management in Petra. *(Photo from the Jane Taylor collection, ACOR Digital Archive.)* Pages 6–7: Camels before the Treasury in Petra. *(Photo courtesy of the Jordan Tourism Board.)*

5. **Excavating and Conserving Umm Al-Jimāl (p. 8):** The double window of House XVIII in Umm Al-Jimāl. This was part of a house built during Byzantine times, which centuries later became an administrative center or caravansarai. Major work at the site, begun by Bert de Vries of Calvin College (now Calvin University), has been undertaken by the Umm el-Jimal Project since 1972. *(Photo by Ali Barkawi, courtesy of the Umm Al-Jimāl Archaeological Project.)*

6. **Fighting Illicit Trafficking of Cultural Heritage (p. 9):** Neolithic (9th–7th millennia BCE) cattle figurine and a figure of the goddess Astarte, returned to Jordan by the United States. *(Photos from the ACOR institutional collection.)*

7. **Surveying Ancient Amman (p. 10):** Aerial view of the Amman Citadel. *(Photo by J. Wilson Myers and Eleanor Myers, from P. M. Bikai [ed.], ACOR: The First 25 Years: The American Center of Oriental Research: 1968–1993 [Amman: ACOR, 1993], p. 23.)*

8. **Advancing the Roman Aqaba Project (p. 11):** Archaeological excavation in the ancient site zone of Aqaba. The project was sponsored by North Carolina State University in affiliation with the American Schools of Oriental Research (now the American Society of Overseas Research) and the American Center of Research. Additional support came from the National Geographic Society, the Joukowsky Family Foundation, the Samuel H. Kress Foundation, the Kyle-Kelso Foundation, the University of Helsinki Institute of Classics, and the IBM Corporation, among others. *(Photo courtesy of the Roman Aqaba Project.)*

9. **Founding the Binational Fulbright Commission (p. 12):** HRH Prince El Hassan bin Talal at the inauguration of Fulbright House, 1994. *(Photo courtesy of the Fulbright Commission in Jordan.)*

10. **Endorsing Scholarship and Research (p. 13):** Photographing an ancient Nabataean façade in Petra in 2024 to replicate photographs taken in 1924. *(Photo courtesy of the Fulbright Commission in Jordan.)*

11. **Mapping Desert Kites (p. 14):** Aerial view of animal traps (kites). The project is being undertaken by Austin Chad Hill of the University of Pennsylvania and Yorke Rowan of the University of Chicago, with the support and engagement of many others. *(Photo by Austin Chad Hill, courtesy of the Kites in Context Project.)*

12. **Studying the Ancient Eastern Deserts (p. 15):** Upper left: Some of the mesas that rise in the Wadi al-Qattafi in Jordan's Black Desert. *(Photo by Austin Chad Hill, courtesy of the Wadi al-Qattafi Survey Project.)* Lower right: Structure SS-11 (Late Neolithic, c. 6500–6000 BCE) on one of the mesas in Wadi al-Qattafi. *(Photo by Gary Rollefson, courtesy of the Eastern Badia Project.)* The Eastern Badia Archaeological Project has been undertaken by Dartmouth College, the University of Chicago and the University of Pennsylvania.

13. **Establishing the First Digital Database of Sites in the Region (p. 16):** Development of the Jordan Antiquities Database and Information System (JADIS) in the 1990s. *(Photo from the ACOR institutional collection.)*

14. **Creating a National Inventory for Jordan's Heritage (p. 17):** The "Goddess of Hayyan" found at the Temple of the Winged Lions in Petra. *(Photo from the Jane Taylor collection, ACOR Digital Archive.)*

15. **Improving Tourism Amenities (p. 18):** View toward the southern theater and the temple

of Zeus from the propylaeum of the sanctuary of Zeus, Jerash. Significant work has been carried out here by the Institut français de Proche Orient (IFPO) with funding from the French Ministry of Foreign Affairs and the World Monuments Fund. *(Photo courtesy of the Jordan Tourism Board.)*

16. **Enhancing Access to Mount Nebo (p. 19):** *Brazen Serpent*, a sculpture by Italian sculptor Giovanni Fantoni. Archaeological work on Mount Nebo has been undertaken by the Studium Biblicum Franciscanum. *(Photo courtesy of the Jordan Tourism Board.)*

17. **Providing Access to the Inaccessible (pp. 20–21):** Main photo: Drone photo of Wadi Rum taken in 2021 for heritage impact and environmental impact assessment reports submitted to the UNESCO World Heritage Center. Three missions for the reports were conducted under the supervision of Tarek Abulhawa, Ehab Eid, and Ahmad Lash, with the USAID-funded Sustainable Cultural Heritage through Engagement of Local Communities Project. *(Photo from the USAID SCHEP collection, ACOR Digital Archive.)* Inset: Camel following a track in Wadi Rum. *(Photo by Yusuf Ahmed, from the USAID SCHEP collection, ACOR Digital Archive.)*

18. **Diving into Jordan's Maritime Heritage (p. 22):** Underwater archaeological survey at Ayla (modern Aqaba). JREDS undertook the Discover the Depth of Aqaba Marine Heritage Project with USAID SCHEP and underwater archaeologists Sawsan Al Fakhri and Islam Sleim. *(Video still image courtesy of JREDS.)*

19. **Discovering an Islamic Port City (p. 23):** Portions of Islamic Aqaba's interior city walls and living, prayer, and work spaces. The Aqaba Project was initially undertaken by Donald Whitcomb of the University of Chicago. Other funding was provided by the National Geographic Society and others. *(Photo by Abed Al Fatah Ghareeb, from the USAID SCHEP collection, ACOR Digital Archive.)*

20. **Preserving Urban Archaeology (p. 24):** The Roman-era Amman Nymphaeum and the Amman River before the river was converted into an underground watercourse in the 1960s. Work on the U.S.-funded restoration of the nymphaeum was performed by professionals and by students from the University of Jordan, Petra University, and the Hashemite University. *(Photo courtesy of the Jordan Tourism Board.)*

21. **Documenting Early Hashemite Built History (p. 25):** A view of Amman from the Roman theater in the 1990s. *Old Houses of Jordan*, which features the photography of Bill Lyons, was written by Mohammad al-Asad and published in 1997 by Turab, the publishing house of the Jordanian Royal Aal Al-Bayt Institute for Islamic Thought. *(Photo by Bill Lyons, courtesy of the Jordan Tourism Board.)*

22. **Discovering the Origins of Art (p. 26):** Main photo: Neolithic human figure found at 'Ain Ghazal made from lime plaster applied to an armature of reeds. *(Photo from the Jane Taylor collection, ACOR Digital Archive.)* Inset: Excavation of another of the human statues, 1983. Work at the site was undertaken by Gary O. Rollefson, then of San Diego State University, Zeidan Kafafi of Yarmouk University, and Alan H. Simmons of the University of Nevada at Las Vegas. *(Photo from the Rami G. Khouri collection, ACOR Digital Archive.)*

23. **Supporting Growth in the Arts (p. 27):** Creation of a mosaic, modeled after a Byzantine "tree of life," at the Madaba Institute for Mosaic Art and Restoration (MIMAR). MIMAR is a nonprofit owned by the Jordanian government and came about through cooperation between the Ministry of Tourism and Antiquities and the Department of Antiquities with support from USAID's Jordan Tourism Development Project and the Italian Government. *(Photo by Abed Al Fatah Ghareeb, from the USAID SCHEP collection, ACOR Digital Archive.)*

24. **Conserving Desert Castles (p. 28):** Main photo: The Umayyad fortified pleasure palace of Qusayr Amra. Its ongoing conservation is a project of the World Monuments Fund (WMF), the Istituto Superiore per la Conservazione ed il Restauro (Italy), and the Department of Antiquities. Earlier efforts were by the Archaeological Museum of Madrid and the University of Granada. *(Photo courtesy of the Jordan Tourism Board.)* Inset: Detail of a ceiling fresco. *(Photo by Zaid Kashour, from the USAID SCHEP collection, ACOR Digital Archive.)*

25. **Understanding Life in the Desert (p. 29):** Qasr Harrana, a desert castle in Jordan's Eastern Badia. The Archaeological and Tourism Reality in the Eastern Desert was written by Ahmad Lash and Wessam Essed. *(Photo courtesy*

of the Jordan Tourism Board.)
26. **Conserving an Umayyad Palace (pp. 30–31):** Qasr Al-Mushatta. It was excavated by the Department of Antiquities. *(Main photo from the Jane Taylor collection, ACOR Digital Archive; inset photo courtesy of the Jordan Tourism Board.)*
27. **Excavating Crusader Castles (pp. 30–31):** Karak Castle. Over the decades, U.S. government funding and American expertise, in collaboration with Jordanian and international colleagues, have contributed to helping excavate and preserve these imposing structures. *(Photo courtesy of the Department of Antiquities of Jordan.)*
28. **Preserving Petra's Temple of the Winged Lions (pp. 32–33):** Main photo: The Temple of the Winged Lions and the glass sign allowing visitors to view a reconstruction. Initial work at the temple was undertaken by Philip Hammond and the American Expedition to Petra, followed by the TWL Initiative, founded by Christopher Tuttle in collaboration with the Department of Antiquities of Jordan and the Petra Development and Tourism Region Authority (PDTRA) and then the USAID-funded Sustainable Cultural Heritage Through Engagement of Local Communities Project. ACOR published two volumes on the temple with funding from the NEH. *(Photo from the USAID SCHEP collection.)* Upper inset: One of the winged-lion column capitals. *(Photo from the P. C. Hammond/American Expedition to Petra archive, ACOR.)* Lower inset: Conservators Wadj Nawafleh and Ageleh Jmeidi and their tools. *(Photo from the USAID SCHEP collection, ACOR Digital Archive.)*
29. **Safeguarding Byzantine Heritage Sites (pp. 32–33):** Shelter over the floor mosaics of the Burnt Palace in the western portion of the Madaba Archaeological Park. Excavation had been carried out by Cherie Lenzen and Ghazi Bisheh. The Madaba Mosaic School, ACOR conservators overseen by Pierre M. Bikai, and the Studium Biblicum Franciscanum conducted restoration work on the mosaics. *(Photo courtesy of the Jordan Tourism Board.)*
30. **Preserving the "Founder's Tomb" in Ancient Capitolias (pp. 34–35):** Conservation of the frescos in the main chamber of the tomb. The Bayt Ras Consortium, which excavated and conserved the tomb, comprises the Department of Antiquities of Jordan, the American Center of Research (ACOR), the USAID-funded Sustainable Cultural Heritage through Engagement of Local Communities Project, the Istituto Superiore per la Conservazione ed il Restauro (Italy), the Istituto Superiore per la Protezione e la Ricerca Ambientale (Italy), the French National Center for Scientific Research (CNRS), and the Institut français du Proche Orient (IFPO), Amman. *(Photo from the USAID SCHEP collection, ACOR Digital Archive.)*
31. **Recording Local Traditions for Future Generations (p. 36):** Bedouin gathered to listen to a rebab, a single-stringed instrument. Donald O. Henry of the University of Tulsa performed the study funded by the National Endowment for the Humanities. *(Photo courtesy of the Jordan Tourism Board.)*
32. **Preserving Intangible Heritage (p. 37):** Dancers and musicians from Jerash performing during the closing ceremony of the Mallol project, in which youth from Jerash learned traditional songs. The project was initiated by Tajalla for Music and Arts Society in Partnership with the Politics and Society Institute. *(Photo from the USAID SCHEP collection, ACOR Digital Archive.)*
33. **Supporting Foundational Research and Discoveries (pp. 38–39):** Ihsan Abd'al Kader and family, Nancy Coinman, Deborah Olszewski, and Nabil Beg'ain of the Wadi al-Hasa project. Work at Wadi el-Hasa has also been funded by the Social Sciences and Humanities Research Council of Canada, St. Francis Xavier University, and the Pennsylvania Museum of Archaeology and Anthropology. *(Photo courtesy of Geoffrey Clark.)*
34. **Providing Digital Resources in a Technological Age (pp. 38–39):** Screenshot of search results for "Taylor" in the ACOR Digital Archive. *(Screenshot from ACOR.)*
35. **Creating Accessible Tourism (p. 40):** Mural depicting a timeline at the entrance to the Busayra archaeological site. *(Photo by Abed Al Fatah Ghareeb, from the USAID SCHEP collection, ACOR Digital Archive.)*
36. **Supporting Small Businesses (p. 41):** Graphic, upper left: Map of the Amman Citadel tourist trail. *(Graphic by Ahmad Qaiseh, USAID SCHEP.)* Photo, upper right: Example of a sign along the trail. Photos, below, left to right: Some of the business proprietors aided by the program: Ayyad Ayyad, Amman Panorama Gallery; Rafa Raed, Jewelry + Henna; Maysoon Shanter, salads; Saeed Shanter, sweets.

(Photos from the USAID SCHEP collection, ACOR Digital Archive.)

37. **Highlighting the Medieval Sugar Factory in Ghor as-Safi (p. 42):** Early in the excavation of the sugar boiling and curing area of the factory. Excavations here by Kontantinos D. Politis have been supported by the Hellenic Society for Near Eastern Studies. *(Photo by Zaid Kashour, USAID SCHEP, ACOR Digital Archive.)*

38. **Uncovering History at Tall al-'Umayri (p. 43):** Aerial view of Tall al-'Umayri with the adjacent Airport Road. The Madaba Plains Project — a consortium of La Sierra University, Andrews University, Canadian University College, Mount Royal University, Pacific Union College, and Walla Walla University — has excavated here through the years. *(Photo by David Kennedy, courtesy of APAAME/ Aerial Photographic Archive for Archaeology in the Middle East.)*

39. **Illuminating the "Dark Ages" (p. 44):** Main photo: The Byzantine church in Petra. ACOR's conservation of the church and its mosaics, performed in close partnership with the Petra Authority and the Department of Antiquities of Jordan, was also supported by many other organizations and private donors. *(Photo from the Rami Khouri collection, ACOR Digital Archive.)* Inset, left: Detail of the mosaic floor. *(Photo from the ACOR Digital Archive.)* Inset, right: Detail of one of the papyri, a 6th-century tax receipt, found in the church. Support for study of the papyri came from USAID, the National Endowment for the Humanities, the University of Michigan, the Academy of Finland, the University of Helsinki, the Ministry of Culture and Education of Finland, the United States Information Agency (USIA), and many other organizations and individuals. *(Photo from Jaako Frösén et al., The Petra Papyri I [Amman: ACOR, 2002], pl. XXV [detail].)*

40. **Enhancing Understanding of the Ancient Kingdoms of Jordan (p. 45):** Aerial view of the Moabite site of Balu'a. The National Science Foundation-sponsored Role of Agriculture in the Development of Social Complexity project, undertaken by Geoffrey Hedges-Knyrim of the University of Connecticut, is part of the Balu'a Regional Archaeological Project, which is sponsored by La Sierra University, Theologische Hochschule Friedensau, and St. Bernard's School of Theology and Ministry, with additional support from Walla Walla University and Sacred Heart Seminary and School of Theology. *(Photo courtesy of APAAME/ Aerial Photographic Archive for Archaeology in the Middle East.)*

41. **Excavating Pella, Hub of the Ancient World (pp. 45–47):** On the hill, the Byzantine church in Pella; in the foreground, the small Roman theater. Work at Pella has been conducted recently by the University of Sydney's Pella Project and was formerly done in cooperation with the College of Wooster. *(Photo courtesy of the Jordan Tourism Board.)*

42. **Fostering Intellectual Exchange (p. 48):** Upper: Participants in the 10th International Conference on the History and Archaeology of Jordan (ICHAJ) at the George Washington University, May 2007. *(Photo by Marvin T. Jones, ACOR.)* Lower: Participants at ICHAJ 14, held in Florence, Italy, January 2019. *(Photo from the USAID SCHEP collection, ACOR.)* Many organizations support each conference.

43. **Elevating Standards of Tourism (p. 49):** Participants in a USAID-funded Pathways to Professionalism program. Vocational training programs that enhance skills and create new pathways for success in the hospitality industry *(Photo courtesy of Chemonics International, Inc.)*

44. **Interpreting History through Ceramics (p. 50):** Above: Assemblage of pottery from a late Hellenistic farmstead at 'Umayri. *(Photo courtesy of the Madaba Plains Project.)* Below: Covers of the English and Arabic editions of Jehad Haron and Douglas R. Clark (eds.), *The Pottery of Jordan: A Manual* (Amman: ACOR, 2022). This book was the result of contributions by many scholars from many countries and institutions. *(Images courtesy of ACOR.)*

45. **Preserving the Palace at Iraq al-Amir (p. 51):** The Hellenistic palace known as Qasr al-Abd ("Castle of the Slave") at Iraq al-Amir. Recent preservation efforts have been undertaken by the Greater Amman Municipality, and the Institut français de Proche Orient (IFPO) also works here. *(Photo from the Jane Taylor collection, ACOR Digital Archive.)*

46. **Reassessing History (p. 52):** An Early Bronze Age IV open-air cult site at Khirbet Iskander. Work at the site, under the direction of Suzanne Richard and Jesse C. Long, Jr., has been supported by Gannon University,

Lubbock Christian University, and McMurray University. *(Photo courtesy of Suzanne Richard.)*

47. **Conserving a Temple of Artemis (p. 53):** The temple of Artemis at Jerash (ancient Gerasa). The Italian Archaeological Expedition at Jerash has been active in the city for many years, and conservation of the site was undertaken by Monumenta Orientalia (Rome). *(Photo from the Jane Taylor collection, ACOR Digital Archive.)*

48. **Founding a New Natural Heritage Museum (p. 54):** Main photo: Display of botanical specimens, with avian taxidermy mounts in the background (right), in the Al-Hussein Bin Talal University Natural Science Museum, first conceptualized by Prof. Jebreel Khoshman, dean of the Faculty of Science. *(Photo by Shatha Abu Aballi, ACOR.)* Inset: Caucasian squirrel (*Sciurus anomalus*) mount in the museum. *(Photo by Abed Al Fatah Ghareeb, USAID SCHEP, ACOR.)*

49. **Maintaining a Public Research Library (p. 55).** Upper: The entrance of the American Center of Research (ACOR). Lower: ACOR's library. ACOR receives support from many private donors around the world, and its projects have received grants from many U.S. and international governmental and other organizations. *(Photos by Pearce Paul Creasman, ACOR.)*

50. **Sustaining Cultural Heritage through Engagement of Local Communities (pp. 56–57):** Activities supported by the USAID-funded Sustainable Cultural Heritage Through Engagement of Local Communities Project, implemented by the American Center of Research (ACOR). Upper, left: Field-recording trainings. *(Photo by Zaid Kashour, USAID SCHEP, ACOR.)* Upper, middle: Dancers at the closing festival of the Mallol project. *(Photo from the USAID SCHEP collection, ACOR Digital Archive.)* Upper, right: Safi Kitchen, a local food and tourism experience that preserves local culture and natural resources, was supported by the project. *(Photo from USAID SCHEP, ACOR.)* Lower, left: Children painting a mural for the Amman Citadel Tourist Trail. *(Photo from the USAID SCHEP collection, ACOR Digital Archive.)* Lower, right: Experiential learning, making ceramics from local materials. *(Photo by Abed Al Fatah Ghareeb, USAID SCHEP, ACOR.)* SCHEP partnered with many other organizations and individuals to achieve its goals.

51. **Building a Rest House at Pella (pp. 58–59):** The rest house in Pella. Ammar Khammash designed the building. *(Photo from the Rami G. Khouri collection, ACOR Digital Archive.)*

52. **Supporting Ecotourism (pp. 58–59):** The Dana Nature Reserve. The Royal Society for the Conservation of Nature (Jordan) manages the reserve and has received funding from diverse Jordanian and international sources. *(Photo from the Jane Taylor collection, ACOR Digital Archive.)*

53. **Revitalizing Water Management in Petra (pp. 60):** Rock-cut reservoir no. 72, cut into the rock southwest of the Bab el-Siq (the entrance to Petra) to collect rainwater. Among the many organizations and scholars supporting study and preservation of Petra's ancient waterworks are UNESCO, John Oleson of the University of Victoria, Daniel Plekhov (Brown University), Catreena Hamarneh (German Protestant Institute of Archaeology), Zeidoun Al-Muheisen (Yarmouk University), and Charles R. Ortloff (CFD Consultants International and the University of Chicago). *(Photo from the Rami G. Khouri collection, ACOR Digital Archive.)*

54. **Conserving the Longest Tunnel of the Classical World (p. 61):** Main photo: the aqueduct tunnel below Gadara/Umm Qais. It was recently studied by Atef Al Shiyab and Hussein Al-Sababha of Yarmouk University and Firas Alawneh of the Hashemite University. *(Photo courtesy of the Jordan Tourism Board.)* Inset: Basalt columns of the octagonal central hall of a 5th-century Byzantine basilica in the city. Excavation of the church was undertaken by the German Protestant Institute at Amman. *(Photo by Bashar Tabbah, from* Unique and Outstanding: Jordan's World Heritage Sites *by HRH Princess Dana Firas [Amman: ICOMOS, Jordan, 2022], courtesy of and copyright ICOMOS Jordan.)*

55. **Developing and Diversifying Tourism Products (p. 62):** Church at the Baptism Site, "Bethany beyond the Jordan." The USAID-funded Building Economic Sustainability through Tourism (BEST) project, undertaken by Chemonics International and involving many partner organizations, helped make improvements to services at this site and many others in Jordan. *(Photo courtesy of Chemonics International, Inc.)*